T0012477

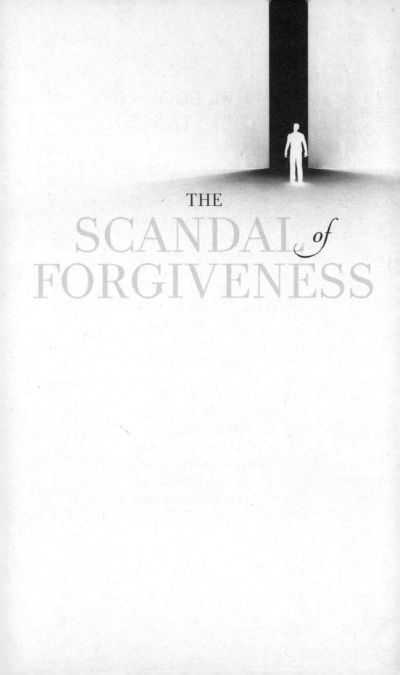

THE
SCANDAL *of*
FORGIVENESS

OTHER BOOKS BY PHILIP YANCEY

Fearfully and Wonderfully
Vanishing Grace
What's So Amazing About Grace?
Prayer: Does It Make Any Difference?
The Jesus I Never Knew
Disappointment with God
Where Is God When It Hurts?
The Gift of Pain
The Question that Never Goes Away
What Good Is God?
Grace Notes
A Skeptic's Guide to Faith
Soul Survivor
Meet the Bible
Reaching for the Invisible God
The Bible Jesus Read
Church: Why Bother?
Finding God in Unexpected Places
I Was Just Wondering
The NIV Student Bible

THE
SCANDAL *of*
FORGIVENESS

Grace Put to the Test

PHILIP
YANCEY

ZONDERVAN®

ZONDERVAN

The Scandal of Forgiveness

Copyright © 2021 by Philip D. Yancey

Portions of this book adapted from *What's So Amazing About Grace*
(978-0-310-21327-7, © 1997).

Requests for information should be addressed to:
Zondervan, *3900 Sparks Dr. SE, Grand Rapids, Michigan 49546*

ISBN 978-0-310-12008-7 (hardcover)
ISBN 978-0-310-12009-4 (ebook)

Any internet addresses (websites, blogs, etc.) and telephone numbers in this
book are offered as a resource. They are not intended in any way to be or imply
an endorsement by Zondervan, nor does Zondervan vouch for the content of
these sites and numbers for the life of this book.

No part of this publication may be reproduced, stored in a retrieval system, or
transmitted in any form or by any means—electronic, mechanical, photocopy,
recording, or any other—except for brief quotations in printed reviews, without
the prior permission of the publisher.

All Scripture quotations, unless otherwise indicated, are taken from the Holy
Bible, New International Version®, NIV®. Copyright © 1973, 1978, 1984, 2011 by
Biblica, Inc.™ Used by permission. All rights reserved worldwide.

Zondervan titles may be purchased in bulk for educational, business,
fundraising, or sales promotional use. For information, please email
SpecialMarkets@Zondervan.com.

Cover Design: Jamie DeBruyn
Cover Photography: Mopic, Shutterstock
Interior Design: Emily Ghattas

Printed in the United States of America

21 22 23 24 25   LSC   10 9 8 7 6 5 4 3 2

CONTENTS

Chapter 1

SET FREE

My friend Mark lives in a middle-class suburban home with his wife and two teenage children. One day he was discussing with his wife whether it was time to put their aging cat to sleep. Something she said struck a nerve, and before he knew it, he was yelling at her. Feeling threatened by his angry outburst, she reached for their landline phone and dialed 911. Mark quickly grabbed the phone from her and unplugged it. Still smoldering, he stalked out of the room, believing the incident was over—until a short time later, when the doorbell rang.

Wearing only boxer shorts and a T-shirt, Mark opened the front door to find two uniformed officers. The 911 call center had detected the aborted call and alerted local police to a possible emergency. Mark tried to explain that everything was fine, that a disagreement had just gotten a little heated, but the police informed him they had a strict protocol for handling potential domestic violence situations. With curious neighbors looking on, they hand-cuffed Mark and escorted him in his underwear to their squad car. He spent that night in jail until his father bailed him out the next morning.

My friend, humiliated, was sentenced to a fourteen-week course in anger management. He found himself in a room with repeat offenders who had expressed their anger with fists, not just words. "Your first assignment is to write an apology to the person you hurt," said the woman conducting the course. Mark took the pen and paper she offered and returned to his seat, only to look around and see that he was the only one who had agreed. The other men glared at him.

When Mark finished writing the apology, the leader thanked him and reduced his sentence. Even then, none of the others followed his lead. "No f-ing way!" one guy said, and the others nodded their approval.

It has taken Mark months to regain his wife's trust. He told me this story, which he was recounting to all his close friends, as part of that effort, for the very reason that it exposed his anger problem. "My first instinct was to dismiss what happened as a ridiculous overreaction to a normal marital dispute. But then I saw how badly I had hurt my wife. If I don't face the ugly truth about myself, and sincerely make amends, I may never earn her forgive-ness, which I need desperately in order to put my family back together."

What he said next has stayed with me: "I don't know

which is harder: for me to apologize or my wife to forgive." Both acts go against all our self-protective instincts. On the one hand, if we've done a wrong, we tend to rationalize away our mistake, blaming the other party, or stress, or a hundred possible psychological reasons that may have led us to act the way we did. On the other hand, if we're the wronged party, we want to nurse our wounds, harbor resentment, and insist on some kind of restitution.

A conflict like Mark's links the two parties with a force almost the opposite of love, one that pulls them apart rather than together. On both sides of the standoff, a thick wall of self-protection goes up. Yet, as if to add insult to injury, only the forgiving party, the wronged one, has the ability to dismantle that wall. Mark could write an apology every day of the year, but his wife alone holds the key to restoration.

"Everyone says forgiveness is a lovely idea," writes C. S. Lewis in *Mere Christianity*—"Until they have something to forgive."

In truth, we all have something to forgive, for human beings will let you down. Parents who make mistakes in rearing you, friends who grow distant, a spouse who irritates and confounds you, church members who judge you—no one loves perfectly, and no one satisfies the need for acceptance that we all long for. Every lasting relationship includes times of disappointment, and sometimes betrayal.

Others may let us down, but the bitterness that results

is something we cultivate in ourselves. Forgiveness represents the only remedy. In the pages that follow you'll encounter stories of forgiveness done well, and forgiveness resisted at any cost. Stores of those who passed the grace test, and those who failed. The stakes are high, for rancor can pass down through generations, promoting enmity within families and even between nations.

In a cruel irony, a refusal to forgive works its negative energy most powerfully in the wronged party. Archbishop Desmond Tutu, a master of forgiveness, describes the process:

> To forgive is not just to be altruistic; in my view it is the best form of self-interest. The process of forgiving does not exclude hatred and anger. These emotions are all part of being human. When I talk of forgiveness I mean the ability to let go of the right to revenge and to slip the chains of rage that bind you to the person who harmed you. When you forgive you are free of the hatred and anger that locks you in a state of victimhood. If you can find it in yourself to forgive, you can move on, and you may even help the perpetrator to become a better person.

On a BBC program first broadcast in 2013, I heard a dramatic account of the process Tutu describes. It told the story of Natascha Kampusch, a ten-year-old Austrian girl who was abducted on the way to school by a man in his mid-thirties. He locked her in a dark, dungeon-like room underneath his garage, where he kept her for eight years. After a while he would let her out to cook for him and do household chores, always under close guard, before locking her in the concrete room each night. At times he beat her so badly that she could hardly walk. He also raped her.

When Natascha finally escaped to a neighbor's house, as an eighteen-year-old, she weighed about the same (105 pounds) as when she entered. Despite the horrific ordeal, she came to a place of forgiveness. As she explained on the program, "I felt I had to forgive him. Only by doing so could I push it away from myself. If I hadn't been able to forgive him then these feelings of frustration and anger would have continued to eat away at me and would have lived on—this entire experience would have continued to live on inside me. It is as if he would have won in the end if I had let that get to me. I didn't want hate to poison me because hate always backfires, it comes back on yourself."

With her typical bluntness, the author Anne Lamott says, "Not forgiving is like taking rat poison and waiting for the rat to die." She elaborates, "Forgiveness means it finally becomes unimportant that you hit back. You're done. It doesn't necessarily mean that you want to have lunch with the person."

Forgiveness is hard enough when the wounding party apologizes, as my friend Mark did, but in Natascha's case her captor showed no sign of repentance. Rather, he killed himself by jumping in front of a train when he learned that police were on his trail. Yet Natascha still felt the need to forgive him as a way of setting herself free from the horrors of the past.

Should someone be forgiven who has not asked for it or admitted the need? Christians have the stunning example of Jesus who, in his first words from the cross, said "Father, forgive them, for they do not know what they are doing." By any reasonable standard of fairness, such a statement is absurd. Crude soldiers were mocking an innocent man even as they drove nails through his wrists and feet and gambled for his clothes. Forgive such people? That scene more than any other exposes the illogic of grace, the motivating force behind forgiveness.

"You have heard that it was said, 'Love your neighbor and hate your enemy,' Jesus had told his followers, reiterating the common rule of human conduct. "But I tell you, love your enemies and pray for those who persecute you . . ." No doubt such words produced shocked and puzzled expressions on the faces of his listeners, and immediately Jesus gave the reason behind his strange command: "that you may be children of your Father in heaven. He causes his sun to rise on the evil and the good, and sends rain on the righteous and the unrighteous."

As God's image-bearers, we are charged with the task of showing the world what God is like. I cannot imagine a more effective way of doing so than following Jesus' example. We who deserve God's wrath receive God's love; we who deserve God's punishment receive God's forgiveness. And if we mirror that pattern in our human relationships, we reveal to the world the likeness of God.

The theologian N. T. Wright makes the intriguing observation that because of the forgiveness brought about by Jesus' reconciling work, "God will not only release the world from its burden of guilt but will also, so to speak, release himself from the burden of always having to be angry with a world gone wrong."

Using vivid metaphors, the Old Testament spells out the scope of God's forgiveness. God removes our offenses from us "as far as the east is from the west" (Psalm 103:12). With an ability unavailable to mere humans, God blots them out "and remembers your sins no more" (Isaiah 43:25). "I have swept away your offenses like a cloud, your sins like the morning mist," God declares (Isaiah 44:22). The prophet Micah depicts God treading our misdeeds underfoot and hurling them into the depths of the sea (Micah 7:19).

We are not God, and have not the capacity to blot out memory. By an act of will, I can forgive, but I can't so easily forget, even when I want to. At this very moment I could compile a list of people who have hurt me, disappointed me, betrayed me. Even after I have gone through the steps of forgiveness, I can still summon up the painful memories and recall them like old wounds. Memories lurk in my brain, and when they surface I must bring them before God and ask for a measure of supernatural grace.

For us humans, forgiveness does not erase the past. Rather, it opens up a new future by blocking the past from poisoning that future. Forgiveness means accepting that the past cannot be changed while trusting God for a better future.

I think of Mark, free at last to pursue a loving marriage. And Natascha, free to carve out a new life. I think of Jesus' disciple Peter, a traitor, now chosen by Jesus to "feed my sheep." I think of Saul of Tarsus, formerly a bounty hunter of Christians, now free to become the greatest missionary of all time.

We should have no illusions about forgiveness, for it may be the most demanding act in human relationships, the hardest thing we ever do. But for anyone who lives and loves imperfectly—in other words, for all of us— forgiveness offers an alternative to an endless cycle of resentment and revenge. It alone can set us free.

Chapter 2

LOVESICK
FATHER

A young girl grows up on a cherry orchard just above Traverse City, Michigan. Her parents, a bit old-fashioned, tend to overreact to her nose ring, the music she listens to, and the length of her skirts. They ground her a few times, and she seethes inside. "I hate you!" she screams at her father when he knocks on the door of her room after an argument, and that night she acts on a plan she has mentally rehearsed scores of times. She runs away.

She has visited Detroit only once before, on a bus trip with her church youth group to watch the Tigers play. Because newspapers in Traverse City report in lurid detail the gangs, the drugs, and the violence in downtown Detroit, she concludes that is probably the last place her parents will look for her. California, maybe, or Florida, but not Detroit.

Her second day there she meets a man who drives the biggest car she's ever seen. He offers her a ride, buys her lunch, arranges a place for her to stay. He gives her some pills that make her feel better than she's ever felt before. She was right all along, she decides: her parents were keeping her from all the fun.

The good life continues for a month, two months, a year. The man with the big car—she calls him "Boss"—teaches her a few things that men like. Since she's underage, men pay a premium for her. She lives in a penthouse, and orders room service whenever she wants. Occasionally she thinks about the folks back home, but their lives now seem so boring and provincial that she can hardly believe she grew up there.

She has a brief scare when she sees her picture printed on the back of a milk carton with the headline "Have you seen this child?" But by now she has blond hair, and with all the makeup and body-piercing jewelry she wears, nobody would mistake her for a child. Besides, most of her friends are runaways, and nobody squeals in Detroit.

After a year the first sallow signs of illness appear, and it amazes her how fast the boss turns mean. "These days, we can't mess around," he growls, and before she knows it she's out on the street without a penny to her name. She still turns a couple of tricks a night, but they don't pay much, and all the money goes to support her habit. When winter blows in she finds herself sleeping on metal grates outside the big department stores. "Sleeping" is the wrong word—a teenage girl at night in downtown Detroit can never relax her guard. Dark bands circle her eyes. Her cough worsens.

One night as she lies awake listening for footsteps, all of a sudden everything about her life looks different. She no longer feels like a woman of the world. She feels like a little girl, lost in a cold and frightening city. She begins to whimper. Her pockets are empty and she's hungry. She needs a fix. She pulls her legs tight underneath her and shivers under the newspapers she's piled atop her coat. Something jolts a synapse of memory and a single image fills her mind: of May in Traverse City, when a million cherry trees bloom at once, with her golden retriever dashing through the rows and rows of blossomy trees in chase of a tennis ball.

God, why did I leave, she says to herself, and pain stabs at her heart. *My dog back home eats better than I do now*. She's sobbing, and she knows in a flash that more than anything else in the world she wants to go home.

Three straight phone calls, three straight connections with the answering machine. She hangs up without leaving a message the first two times, but the third time she says, "Dad, Mom, it's me. I was wondering about maybe coming home. I'm catching a bus up your way, and it'll get there about midnight tomorrow. If you're not there, well, I guess I'll just stay on the bus until it hits Canada."

It takes about seven hours for a bus to make all the stops between Detroit and Traverse City, and during that time she realizes the flaws in her plan. What if her parents are out of town and miss the message? Shouldn't she have waited another day or so until she could talk to them? And even if they are home, they probably wrote her off as dead long ago. She should have given them some time to overcome the shock.

Her thoughts bounce back and forth between those worries and the speech she is preparing for her father. "Dad, I'm sorry. I know I was wrong. It's not your fault; it's all mine. Dad, can you forgive me?" She says the words over and over, her throat tightening even as she rehearses them. She hasn't apologized to anyone in years.

The bus has been driving with lights on since Bay City. Tiny snowflakes hit the pavement rubbed worn by thousands of tires, and the asphalt steams. She's forgotten how dark it gets at night out here. A deer darts across the road and the bus swerves. Every so often, a billboard. A sign posting the mileage to Traverse City. *Oh, God.*

When the bus finally rolls into the station, its air brakes hissing in protest, the driver announces in a crackly voice over the microphone, "Fifteen minutes, folks. That's all we have here." Fifteen minutes to decide her life. She checks herself in a compact mirror, smooths her hair, and licks the lipstick off her teeth. She looks at the tobacco stains on her fingertips, and wonders if her parents will notice. If they're there.

She walks into the terminal not knowing what to expect. Not one of the thousand scenes that have played out in her mind prepare her for what she sees. There, in the concrete-walls-and-plastic-chairs bus terminal in Traverse City, Michigan, stands a group of forty brothers and sisters and great-aunts and uncles and cousins and a grandmother and great-grandmother to boot. They're all wearing goofy party hats and blowing noise-makers, and taped across the entire wall of the terminal is a computer-generated banner that reads "Welcome home!"

Out of the crowd of well-wishers breaks her dad. She stares out through the tears quivering in her eyes like hot mercury and begins the memorized speech, "Dad, I'm sorry. I know …"

He interrupts her. "Hush, child. We've got no time for that. No time for apologies. You'll be late for the party. A banquet's waiting for you at home."

We are accustomed to finding a catch in every promise, but Jesus' stories of scandalous forgiveness and extravagant grace include no catch, no loophole disqualifying us from God's love. Each has at its core an ending too good to be true—or so good that it must be true.

How different are these stories from my own childhood notions about God: a God who forgives, yes, but reluctantly, after making the penitent squirm? I imagined God as a distant thundering figure who prefers fear and respect to love. Jesus tells instead of a father publicly humiliating himself by rushing out to embrace a son who has squandered half the family fortune. There is no solemn lecture, "I hope you've learned your lesson!" Instead, Jesus tells of the father's exhilaration—"This my son was dead, and is alive again; he was lost, and is found"— and then adds the buoyant phrase, "they began to make merry."

What blocks forgiveness is not God's reticence—"But while he was still a long way off, his father saw him and was filled with compassion for him"—but ours. God's arms are always extended; we are the ones who turn away.

I have meditated enough on Jesus' stories of grace to let their meaning filter through. Still, each time I confront their astonishing message I realize how thickly the veil of ungrace obscures my view of God. A housewife jumping up and down in glee over the discovery of a lost coin is not what naturally comes to mind when I think of God. Yet that is the image Jesus insisted upon.

The story of the Prodigal Son, after all, appears in a string of three stories by Jesus—the lost sheep, the lost coin, the lost son—all of which seem to make the same point. Each underscores the loser's sense of loss, tells of the thrill of rediscovery, and ends with a scene of jubilation. Jesus says in effect, "Do you want to know what it feels like to be God? When one of those two-legged humans pays attention to me, it feels like I just reclaimed my most valuable possession, which I had given up for lost." To God himself, it feels like the discovery of a lifetime.

Strangely, rediscovery may strike a deeper chord than

discovery. To lose, and then find, a Mont Blanc pen makes the owner happier than the day she got it in the first place. Once, in the days before computers, I lost four chapters of a book I was writing when I left my only copy in a motel room drawer. For two weeks the motel insisted that cleaning personnel had thrown the stack of papers away. I was inconsolable. How could I summon the energy to start all over when for months I had worked at polishing and improving those four chapters? I would never find the same words. Then one day a cleaning woman who spoke little English called to tell me she had not thrown the chapters away after all. Believe me, I felt far more joy over the chapters that were found than I had ever felt in the process of writing them.

That experience gives me a small foretaste of what it must feel like for a parent to get a phone call from the FBI reporting that the daughter abducted six months ago has been located at last, alive. Or for a wife to get a visit from the Army with a spokesman apologizing about the mix up; her husband had not been aboard the wrecked helicopter after all. And those images give a mere glimpse of what it must feel like for the Maker of the Universe to get another member of his family back. In Jesus' words, "In the same way, I tell you, there is rejoicing in the presence of the angels of God over one sinner who repents."

Grace is shockingly personal. As Henri Nouwen points out, "God rejoices. Not because the problems of the world have been solved, not because all human pain and suffering have come to an end, nor because thousands of people have been converted and are now praising him for his goodness. No, God rejoices because *one* of his children who was lost has been found."

In the Academy of Fine Arts in Venice there hangs a painting by Paolo Veronese, a painting that got him in trouble with the Inquisition. The painting depicts Jesus at a banquet with his disciples, complete with Roman soldiers playing in one corner, a man with a bloody nose on the other side, stray dogs roaming around, a few drunks, and also midgets, blackamoors, and anachronistic Huns. Called before the Inquisition to explain these irreverences, Veronese defended his painting by showing from the Gospels that these were the very kinds of people Jesus mingled with. Scandalized, the Inquisitors made him change the title of the painting and make the scene secular rather than religious.

In doing so, of course, the Inquisitors replicated the attitude of the Pharisees in Jesus' day. They too were scandalized by the tax collectors, half-breeds, foreigners, and women of ill repute who hung out with Jesus. They too had trouble swallowing the notion that these are the people God loves. At the very moment Jesus was captivating the crowd with his parables of grace, Pharisees stood at the edges of the crowd muttering and grinding their teeth. In the story of the Prodigal Son, provocatively,

Jesus brought in the older brother to voice proper outrage at his father for rewarding irresponsible behavior. What kind of "family values" would his father communicate by throwing a party for such a renegade? What kind of virtue would that encourage?*

The gospel is not at all what we would come up with on our own. I, for one, would expect to honor the virtuous over the profligate. I would expect to have to clean up my act before even applying for an audience with a Holy God. But Jesus told of God ignoring a fancy religious teacher and turning instead to an ordinary sinner who pleads, "God, have mercy." Throughout the Bible, in fact, God shows a marked preference for "real" people over "good" people. In Jesus' own words, "There will be more rejoicing in heaven over one sinner who repents than over ninety-nine righteous persons who do not need to repent."

In one of his last acts before death, Jesus forgave a thief dangling on a cross, knowing full well the thief had converted out of plain fear. That thief would never study the Bible, never attend synagogue or church, and never make amends to all those he had wronged. He simply said "Jesus, remember me," and Jesus promised, "Today you will be with me in paradise." It was another shocking

---

* The contemporary preacher Fred Craddock once tinkered with details of the parable to make just this point. In a sermon, he had the father slip the ring and robe on the *older* brother, then kill the fatted calf in honor of his years of faithfulness and obedience. A woman in the back of the sanctuary yelled out, "That's the way it *should* have been written!"

reminder that grace does not depend on what we have done for God but rather what God has done for us.

Ask people what they must do to get to heaven and most reply, "Be good." Jesus' stories contradict that answer. All we must do is cry, "Help!" God welcomes home anyone who will have him and, in fact, has made the first move already. Most experts—doctors, lawyers, marriage counselors—set a high value on themselves and wait for clients to come to them. Not God. As Søren Kierkegaard put it,

> When it is a question of a sinner He does not merely stand still, open his arms and say, "Come hither"; no, He stands there and waits, as the father of the lost son waited, rather He does not stand and wait, He goes forth to seek, as the shepherd sought the lost sheep, as the woman sought the lost coin. He goes—yet no, He has gone, but infinitely farther than any shepherd or any woman, He went, in sooth, the infinitely long way from being God to becoming man, and that way He went in search of sinners.

Kierkegaard puts his finger on perhaps the most important aspect of Jesus' parables. They were not merely pleasant stories to hold listeners' attention or literary vessels to hold theological truth. They were, in fact, the template of Jesus' life on earth. He was the shepherd who left the safety of the fold for the dark and dangerous night outside. To his banquets he welcomed tax collectors and reprobates and whores. He came for the sick and not the well, for the unrighteous and not the righteous. And to those who betrayed him—especially the disciples, who forsook him at his time of greatest need—he responded like a lovesick father.

Theologian Karl Barth, after writing thousands of pages in his *Church Dogmatics*, arrived at this simple definition of God: "the One who loves."

Not long ago I heard from a pastor friend who was battling with his fifteen-year-old daughter. He knew she was using birth control, and several nights she had not bothered to come home at all. The parents had tried various forms of punishment, to no avail. The daughter lied to them, deceived them, and found a way to turn the tables on them: "It's your fault for being so strict!"

My friend told me, "I remember standing before the plate-glass window in my living room, staring out into the darkness, waiting for her to come home. I felt such rage. I wanted to be like the father of the Prodigal Son, yet I was furious with my daughter for the way she would manipulate us and twist the knife to hurt us. And of course, she was hurting herself more than anyone. I understood then the passages in the prophets expressing God's anger. The people knew how to wound him, and God cried out in pain.

"And yet I must tell you, when my daughter came home that night, or rather the next morning, I wanted nothing in the world so much as to take her in my arms, to love her, to tell her I wanted the best for her. I was a helpless, lovesick father."

Now, when I think about God, I hold up that image of the lovesick father, which is miles away from the stern monarch I used to envision. I think of my friend standing in front of the plate-glass window gazing achingly into the darkness. I think of Jesus' depiction of the Waiting Father, heartsick, abused, yet wanting above all else to forgive and begin anew, to announce with joy, "This my son was dead, and is alive again; he was lost, and is found."

Mozart's *Requiem* contains a wonderful line that has become my prayer, one I pray with increasing confidence: "Remember, merciful Jesu, That I am the cause of your journey." I think he remembers.

Chapter 3

THE NEW MATH
OF GRACE

By my reckoning Judas and Peter stand out as the most mathematical of the disciples. Judas must have shown some facility with numbers or the others would not have elected him treasurer. Peter was a stickler for detail, always trying to pin down Jesus' precise meaning. Also, the Gospels record that when Jesus engineered a miraculous catch of fish, Peter hauled in 153 big ones. Who but a mathematician would have bothered to count the squirming pile?

It was altogether in character, then, for the scrupulous apostle Peter to pursue some mathematical formula of grace. "How many times shall I forgive my brother when he sins against me?" he asked Jesus. "Up to seven times?" Peter was erring on the side of magnanimity, for the rabbis in his day had suggested three as the maximum number of times one might be expected to forgive.

"Not seven times, but seventy-seven times," replied Jesus in a flash. Some manuscripts have "seventy times seven," but it hardly matters whether Jesus said 77 or 490: forgiveness, he implied, is not the kind of thing you count on an abacus.

Peter's question prompted another of Jesus' trenchant stories, about a servant who has somehow piled up a debt of several million dollars. The fact that realistically no servant could accumulate a debt so huge underscores Jesus' point: confiscating the man's family, children, and all his property would not make a dent in repaying the debt. It is unforgivable. Nevertheless the king, touched with pity, abruptly cancels the debt and lets the servant off scot-free.

Suddenly, the plot twists. The servant who has just been forgiven seizes a colleague who owes him a few dollars and begins to choke him. "Pay back what you owe me!" he demands, and throws the man into jail. In a word, the greedy servant is an *ingrate*.

Why Jesus draws the parable with such exaggerated strokes comes clear when he reveals that the king represents God. This above all should determine our attitude toward others: a humble awareness that God has already forgiven us a debt so mountainous that beside it any person's wrongs against us shrink to the size of anthills. How can we *not* forgive each other in light of all God has forgiven us?

As C. S. Lewis put it, "To be a Christian means to forgive the inexcusable, because God has forgiven the inexcusable in you." Lewis himself fathomed the depths of God's forgiveness in a flash of revelation as he repeated the phrase in the Apostle's Creed, "I believe in the forgiveness of sins," on St. Mark's Day. His sins were gone, forgiven! "This truth appeared in my mind in so clear a light that I perceived that never before (and that after many confessions and absolutions) had I believed it with my whole heart."

The more I reflect on Jesus' parables, the more I like the word "scandalous" to describe the mathematics of the gospel. I believe Jesus gave us these stories about grace in order to call us to step completely outside our tit-for-tat world of ungrace and enter into God's realm of infinite grace. As Miroslav Volf puts it, "the economy of undeserved grace has primacy over the economy of moral deserts."

From nursery school onward we are taught how to succeed in the world of ungrace. The early bird gets the worm. No pain, no gain. There is no such thing as a free lunch. Demand your rights. Get what you pay for. I know these rules well because I live by them. I work for what I earn; I like to win; I insist on my rights. I want people to get what they deserve—nothing more, nothing less.

Yet if I care to listen, I hear a loud whisper from the gospel that I did not get what I deserved. I deserved punishment and got forgiveness. I deserved wrath and got love. I deserved debtors' prison and got instead a clean credit history. I deserved stern lectures and crawl-on-your-knees repentance; I got a banquet spread for me.

In a manner of speaking, grace solves a dilemma for God. You do not have to read far in the Bible to detect an underlying tension in how God feels about humanity. On the one hand, God loves us; on the other hand, our behavior repulses him. God yearns to see in people something of his own image reflected; at best he sees shattered fragments of that image. Still, God cannot—or will not—give up.

A passage from Isaiah is often cited as proof of God's remoteness and power:

> "For my thoughts are not your thoughts,
>   neither are your ways my ways,"
>   declares the LORD.
> "As the heavens are higher than the earth,
>   so are my ways higher than your ways
>   and my thoughts than your thoughts."

In context, though, God is actually describing his eagerness to forgive. The same God who created the heavens and the earth has the power to bridge the great chasm that separates him from his creatures. He will reconcile, he will forgive, no matter what obstacles his prodigal children put in the way. As the prophet Micah says, "You do not stay angry forever but delight to show mercy."

Sometimes God's conflicting emotions tug against each other in the very same scene. In the book of Hosea, for example, God wavers between tender reminiscences of his people and solemn threats of judgment. "Swords will flash in their cities," he warns darkly, and then almost in midsentence a cry of love escapes:

> How can I give you up, Ephraim?
> How can I hand you over, Israel? . . .
> My heart is changed within me;
> all my compassion is aroused.

"I will not carry out my fierce anger," God concludes at last. "For I am God, and not man—the Holy One among you." Once again God reserves the right to alter the rules of retribution. Although Israel has fully earned his rebuff, they will not get what they deserve. *I am God, and not man.* God will go to any preposterous length to get his family back.

In an astonishing acted-out parable, God asks the prophet Hosea to marry a woman named Gomer in order to illustrate his love for Israel. Gomer bears three children for Hosea, then abandons the family to live with another man. For a time she works as a prostitute, and it is during this period that God gives the shocking command to Hosea, "Go, show your love to your wife again, though she is loved by another and is an adulteress. Love her as the LORD loves the Israelites, though they turn to other gods...."

In Hosea, the scandal of forgiveness became an actual, talk-of-the-town scandal. What goes through a man's mind when his wife treats him as Gomer treated Hosea? He wanted to kill her; he wanted to forgive her. He wanted divorce; he wanted reconciliation. She shamed him; she melted him. Absurdly, against all odds, the irresistible power of love won out. Hosea the cuckold, joke of the community, welcomed his wife back home.

Gomer did not get fairness, or even justice; she got grace. Every time I read their story—or read God's speeches that begin with sternness and dissolve into tears—I marvel at a God who allows himself to endure such humiliation only to come back for more. "How can I give you up, Ephraim? How can I hand you over, Israel?" Substitute your own name for Ephraim and Israel. At the heart of the gospel is a God who deliberately surrenders to the wild, irresistible power of love.

Centuries later an apostle would explain God's response in more analytical terms: "But where sin increased, grace increased all the more." Paul knew better than anyone who has ever lived that grace comes undeserved, at God's initiative and not our own. Knocked flat on the ground on the way to Damascus, he never recovered from the impact of grace: the word appears no later than the second sentence in every one of his letters. As Frederick Buechner says, "Grace is the best he can wish them because grace is the best he himself ever received."

Paul harped on grace because he knew what could happen if we believe we have earned God's love. In the dark times, if perhaps we badly fail God, or if for no good reason we simply feel unloved, we would stand on shaky ground. We would fear that God might stop loving us when he discovers the real truth about us. Paul—"The chief of sinners" he once called himself—knew beyond doubt that God loves people because of who God is, not because of who we are.

Aware of the apparent scandal of forgiveness, Paul took pains to explain how God has made peace with human beings. Grace baffles us because it goes against the intuition everyone has that, in the face of injustice, some price must be paid. A murderer cannot simply go free. A child abuser cannot shrug and say, "I just felt like it." Anticipating these objections, Paul stressed that a price has been paid—by God himself. God gave up his own Son rather than give up on humanity.

Grace costs nothing for the recipients but everything for the giver. God's grace is not a grandfatherly display of "niceness," for it cost the exorbitant price of Calvary. "There is only one real law—the law of the universe," said Dorothy Sayers. "It may be fulfilled either by way of judgment or by the way of grace, but it *must* be fulfilled one way or the other." By accepting the judgment in his own body, Jesus fulfilled that law, and God found a way to forgive.

In the movie *The Last Emperor*, the young child anointed as the last emperor of China lives a magical life of luxury with a thousand eunuch servants at his command. "What happens when you do wrong?" his brother asks. "When I do wrong, someone else is punished," the boy emperor replies. To demonstrate, he breaks a jar, and one of the servants is beaten. In Christian theology, Jesus reversed that ancient pattern: when the servants erred, the King was punished. Grace is free only because the giver himself has borne the cost.

When the renowned theologian Karl Barth visited the University of Chicago, students and scholars crowded around him. At a press conference, one asked, "Dr. Barth, what is the most profound truth you have learned in your studies?" Without hesitation he replied, "Jesus loves me, this I know, for the Bible tells me so." I agree with Karl Barth. Why, then, do I so often act as if I am trying to earn that love? Why do I have such trouble accepting it?

As Dr. Bob Smith and Bill Wilson, the founders of Alcoholics Anonymous, first devised their twelve-step program, they went to Bill D., a prominent attorney who had flunked out of eight separate detox programs in six months. Strapped in a hospital bed as punishment for attacking two nurses, Bill D. had no choice but to listen to his visitors, who shared their own stories of addiction and the recent hope they had discovered through belief in a Higher Power.

As soon as they mentioned their Higher Power, Bill D. shook his head sadly. "No, no," he said. "It's too late for me. I still believe in God all right, but I know mighty well that He doesn't believe in me anymore."

Bill D. expressed what many of us feel at times. Weighed down by repeated failures, lost hope, a sense of unworthiness, we pull around ourselves a shell that makes us almost impervious to grace. Like foster children who choose again and again to return to abusive families, we turn stubbornly away from grace.

I know how I respond to rejection letters from magazine editors and to critical letters from readers. I know how high my spirits soar when a larger than expected royalty check arrives, and how low they sink when the check is small. I know that my self-image at the end of the day depends largely on what kind of messages I have received from other people. Am I liked? Am I loved? I await the answers from my friends, my neighbors, my family—like a starving man, I await the answers.

Occasionally, all too occasionally, I sense the truth of grace. There are times when I study the parables and grasp that they are about *me*. I am the sheep the shepherd has left the flock to find, the prodigal for whom the father scans the horizon, the servant whose debt has been forgiven. I am the beloved one of God.

Not long ago I received in the mail a postcard from a friend that had on it only six words, "I am the one Jesus loves." I smiled when I saw the return address, for my strange friend excels at these pious slogans. When I called him, though, he told me the slogan came from the author and speaker Brennan Manning. At a seminar, Manning referred to Jesus' closest friend on earth, the disciple named John, identified in the Gospels as "the one Jesus loved." Manning said, "If John were to be asked, 'What is your primary identity in life?' he would not reply, 'I am a disciple, an apostle, an evangelist, an author of one of the four Gospels,' but rather, 'I am the one Jesus loves.'"

What would it mean, I ask myself, if I too came to the place where I saw my primary identity in life as "the one Jesus loves"? How differently would I view myself at the end of a day?

Sociologists have a theory of the looking-glass self: you become what the most important person in your life (wife, father, boss, etc.) thinks you are. How would my life change if I truly believed the Bible's astounding words about God's love for me, if I looked in the mirror and saw what God sees?

Brennan Manning tells the story of an Irish priest who, on a walking tour of a rural parish, sees an old peasant kneeling by the side of the road, praying. Impressed, the priest says to the man, "You must be very close to God." The peasant looks up from his prayers, thinks a moment, and then smiles, "Yes, he's very fond of me."

God exists outside of time, the theologians tell us. God created time as an artist chooses a medium to work with, and is unbound by it. He sees the future and the past in a kind of eternal present. If right about this property of God, the theologians have helped explain how God can possibly call "beloved" a person as inconstant, fickle, and temperamental as I am. When God looks upon my life graph, he sees not jagged swerves toward good and bad but rather a steady line of good: the goodness of God's Son captured in a moment of time and applied for all eternity.

As the seventeenth-century poet John Donne put it,

> For in the Book of Life, the name of Mary Magdalen was as soon recorded, for all her incontinency, as the name of the blessed Virgin, for all her integrity; and the name of St. Paul, who drew his sword against Christ, as soon as St. Peter, who drew his in defence of him: for the Book of Life was not written successively, word after word, line after line, but delivered as a Print, all together.

I grew up with the image of a mathematical God who weighed my good and bad deeds on a set of scales and always found me wanting. Somehow I missed the God of the Gospels, a God of mercy and generosity who keeps finding ways to shatter the relentless laws of ungrace. God tears up the mathematical tables and introduces the new math of *grace*, the most surprising, twisting, unexpected-ending word in the English language.

Grace makes its appearance in so many forms that I have trouble defining it. I am ready, though, to attempt something like a definition of grace in relation to God. *Grace means there is nothing we can do to make God love us more*—no amount of spiritual calisthenics and renunciations, no amount of knowledge gained from seminaries and divinity schools, no amount of crusading on behalf of righteous causes. *And grace means there is nothing we can do to make God love us less*—no amount of racism or pride or pornography or adultery or even murder. Grace means that God already loves us as much as an infinite God can possibly love.

There is a simple cure for people who doubt God's love and question God's grace: to turn to the Bible and examine the kind of people God loves. Jacob, who dared take God on in a wrestling match and ever after bore a wound from that struggle, became the eponym for God's people, the "children of Israel." The Bible tells of a murderer and adulterer who gained a reputation as the greatest king of the Old Testament, a "man after God's own heart."

And of a church being led by a disciple who cursed and swore that he had never known Jesus. And of a missionary being recruited from the ranks of the Christian-torturers. I get mailings from Amnesty International, and as I look at their photos of men and women who have been beaten and cattle-prodded and jabbed and spit on and electrocuted, I ask myself, "What kind of human being could do that to another human being?" Then I read the book of Acts and meet the kind of person who could do such a thing—now an apostle of grace, a servant of Jesus Christ, the greatest missionary history has ever known. If God can love that kind of person, maybe, just maybe, he can love the likes of me.

I cannot moderate my definition of grace, because the Bible forces me to make it as sweeping as possible. God is "the God of all grace," in the apostle Peter's words. And grace means there is nothing I can do to make God love me more, and nothing I can do to make God love me less. It means that I, even I who deserve the opposite, am invited to take my place at the table in God's family.

Chapter 4

UNBROKEN
CHAIN

In 1898 Daisy was born into a working-class Chicago family, the eighth child of ten. The father barely earned enough to feed them all, and after he took up drinking, money got much scarcer. Daisy, closing in on her hundredth birthday as I write this, shudders when she talks about those days. Her father was a "mean drunk," she says. Daisy used to cower in the corner, sobbing, as he kicked her baby brother and sister across the linoleum floor. She hated him with all her heart.

One day the father declared that he wanted his wife out of the house by noon. All ten kids crowded around their mother, clinging to her skirt and crying, "No, don't go!" But their father did not back down. Holding on to her brothers and sisters for support, Daisy watched through the bay window as her mother walked down the sidewalk, shoulders adroop, a suitcase in each hand, growing smaller and smaller until finally she disappeared from view.

Some of the children eventually rejoined their mother, and some went to live with other relatives. It fell to Daisy to stay with her father. She grew up with a hard knot of bitterness inside her, a tumor of hatred over what he had done to the family. All the kids dropped out of school early in order to take jobs or join the Army, and then one by one they moved away to other towns. They got married, started families, and tried to put the past behind them. The father vanished—no one knew where and no one cared.

Many years later, to everyone's surprise, the father resurfaced. He had guttered out, he said. Drunk and cold, he had wandered into a Salvation Army rescue mission one night. To earn a meal ticket he first had to attend a worship service. When the speaker asked if anyone wanted to accept Jesus, he thought it only polite to go forward along with some of the other drunks. He was more surprised than anybody when the "sinner's prayer" actually worked. The demons inside him quieted down. He sobered up. He began studying the Bible and praying. For the first time in his life he felt loved and accepted. He felt clean.

And now, he told his children, he was looking them up one by one to ask for forgiveness. He couldn't defend anything that had happened. He couldn't make it right. But he was sorry, more sorry than they could possibly imagine.

The children, now middle-aged and with families of their own, were initially skeptical. Some doubted his sincerity, expecting him to fall off the wagon at any moment. Others figured he would soon ask for money. Neither happened, and in time the father won them over, all except Daisy.

Long ago Daisy had vowed never to speak to her father—"That man" she called him—again. Her father's reappearance rattled her badly, and old memories of his drunken rages came flooding back as she lay in bed at night. "He can't undo all that just by saying 'I'm sorry,'" Daisy insisted. She wanted no part of him.

The father may have given up drinking, but alcohol had damaged his liver beyond repair. He got very sick, and for the last five years of his life he lived with one of his daughters, Daisy's sister. They lived, in fact, eight houses down the street from Daisy, on the very same row-house block. Keeping her vow, Daisy never once stopped in to visit her dying father, even though she passed by his house whenever she went grocery shopping or caught a bus.

Daisy did consent to let her own children visit their grandfather. Nearing the end, the father saw a little girl come to his door and step inside. "Oh, Daisy, Daisy, you've come to me at last," he cried, gathering her in his arms. The adults in the room didn't have the heart to tell him the girl was not Daisy, but her daughter Margaret. He was hallucinating grace.

All her life Daisy determined to be unlike her father, and indeed she never touched a drop of alcohol. Yet she ruled her own family with a milder form of the tyranny she had grown up under. She would lie on a couch with a rubber ice pack on her head and scream at the kids to "Shut up!"

"Why did I ever have you stupid kids anyway?" she would yell. "You've ruined my life!" The Great Depression had hit, and each child was one more mouth to feed. She had six in all, rearing them in the two-bedroom row house she lives in to this day. In such close quarters, they seemed always underfoot. Some nights she gave them all whippings just to make a point: she knew they'd done wrong even if she hadn't caught them.

Hard as steel, Daisy never apologized and never forgave. Her daughter Margaret remembers as a child coming in tears to apologize for something she'd done. Daisy responded with a parental catch-22: "You can't possibly be sorry! If you were really sorry, you wouldn't have done it in the first place."

I have heard many such stories of unforgiveness from Margaret, whom I know well. All her life she determined to be different from her mother, Daisy. But Margaret's life had its own tragedies, some large and some small, and as her four children entered their teenage years she felt she was losing control of them. She too wanted to lie on the couch with an ice pack and scream, "Shut up!" She too wanted to whip them just to make a point or maybe to release some of the tension coiled inside her.

Her son Michael, who turned sixteen in the 1960s, especially got under her skin. He listened to rock and roll, wore "granny glasses," let his hair grow long. Margaret kicked him out of the house when she caught him smoking pot, and he moved into a hippie commune. She continued to threaten and scold him. She reported him to a judge. She wrote him out of her will. She tried everything she could think of, and nothing got through to Michael. The words she flung up against him fell back, useless, until finally one day in a fit of anger she said, "I never want to see you again as long as I live." That was twenty-six years ago and she has not seen him since.

Michael is also my close friend. Several times during those twenty-six years I have attempted some sort of reconciliation between the two, and each time I confront again the terrible power of unforgiveness. When I asked Margaret if she regretted anything she had said to her son, if she'd like to take anything back, she turned on me in a flash of hot rage as if I were Michael himself. "I don't know why God didn't take him long ago, for all the things he's done!" she said, with a wild, scary look in her eye.

Her brazen fury caught me off guard. I stared at her for a minute: her hands clenched, her face florid, tiny muscles twitching around her eyes. "Do you mean you wish your own son was dead?" I asked at last. She never answered.

Michael emerged from the sixties mellower, his mind dulled by LSD. He moved to Hawaii, lived with a woman, left her, tried another, left her, and then got married. "Sue is the real thing," he told me when I visited him once. "This one will last."

It did not last. I remember a phone conversation with Michael, interrupted by the annoying technological feature known as "call waiting." The line clicked and Michael said, "Excuse me a second," then left me holding a silent phone receiver for at least four minutes. He apologized when he came back on. His mood had darkened. "It was Sue," he said. "We're settling some of the last financial issues of the divorce."

"I didn't know you still had contact with Sue," I said, making conversation.

"I don't!" he cut in, using almost the same tone I had heard from his mother, Margaret. "I hope I never see her again as long as I live!"

We both stayed silent for a long time. We had just been talking about Margaret, and although I said nothing it seemed to me that Michael had recognized in his own voice the tone of his mother, which was actually the tone of her mother, tracing all the way back to what happened in a Chicago row house nearly a century ago.

Like a spiritual defect encoded in the family DNA, ungrace gets passed on in an unbroken chain.

U ngrace does its work quietly and lethally, like a poisonous, undetectable gas. A father dies unforgiven. A mother who once carried a child in her own body does not speak to that child for half its life. The toxin steals on, from generation to generation.

Margaret is a devout Christian who studies the Bible every day, and once I spoke to her about the parable of the Prodigal Son. "What do you do with that parable?" I asked. "Do you hear its message of forgiveness?"

She had obviously thought about the matter, for without hesitation she replied that the parable appears in Luke 15 as the third in a series of three: lost coin, lost sheep, lost son. She said the whole point of the Prodigal Son is to demonstrate how human beings differ from inanimate objects (coins) and from animals (sheep). "People have free will," she said. "They have to be morally responsible. That boy had to come crawling back on his knees. He had to repent. That was Jesus' point."

That was not Jesus' point, Margaret. All three stories emphasize the *finder's* joy. True, the prodigal returned home of his own free will, but clearly the central focus of the story is the father's outrageous love bestowed on his son through an act of scandalous forgiveness: "But while he was still a long way off, his father saw him and was filled with compassion for him; he ran to his son, threw his arms around him and kissed him." When the son tries to repent, the father interrupts his prepared speech in order to get the celebration under way.

A missionary in Lebanon once read this parable to a group of villagers who lived in a culture very similar to the one Jesus described and who had never heard the story. "What do you notice?" he asked.

Two details of the story stood out to the villagers. First, by claiming his inheritance early, the son was saying to his father, "I wish you were dead!" The villagers could not imagine a patriarch taking such an insult or agreeing to the son's demand. Second, they noticed that the father *ran* to greet his long-lost son. In the Middle East, a man of stature walks with slow and stately dignity; never does he run. In Jesus' story the father runs, and Jesus' audience no doubt gasped at this detail.

Grace is unfair, which is one of the hardest things about it. It is unreasonable to expect a woman to forgive the terrible things her father did to her just because he apologizes many years later, and totally unfair to ask that a mother overlook the many offenses her teenage son committed. Grace, however, is not about fairness.

What is true of families is true also of tribes, races, and nations.

Chapter 5

AN UNNATURAL ACT

Ungrace plays like the background static of life for families, nations, and institutions. It is, sadly, our natural human state.

I once shared a meal with two scientists who had just emerged from the glass-enclosed biosphere near Tucson, Arizona. Four men and four women had volunteered for the two-year isolation experiment. All were accomplished scientists, all had undergone psychological testing and preparation, and all had entered the biosphere fully briefed on the rigors they would face while sealed off from the outside world. The scientists told me that within a matter of months the eight "bionauts" had split into two groups of four, and during the final months of the experiment these two groups refused to speak to each other. Eight people lived in a bubble split in half by an invisible wall of ungrace.

Frank Reed, an American citizen held hostage in Lebanon, disclosed upon his release that he had not spoken to one of his fellow hostages for several months following some minor dispute. Most of that time, the two feuding hostages had been chained together.

Ungrace causes cracks to fissure open between mother and daughter, father and son, brother and sister, between scientists, and prisoners, and tribes, and races. Left alone, cracks widen, and for the resulting chasms of ungrace there is only one remedy: the frail rope-bridge of forgiveness.

In the heat of an argument my wife came up with an acute theological formulation. We were discussing my shortcomings in a rather spirited way when she said, "I think it's pretty amazing that I forgive you for some of the dastardly things you've done!"

Since I'm writing about forgiveness, not sin, I will omit the juicy details of those dastardly things. What struck me about her comment, rather, was its sharp insight into the nature of forgiveness. It is no sweet platonic ideal to be dispersed in the world like air freshener sprayed from a can. Forgiveness is achingly difficult, and long after you've forgiven, the wound—my dastardly deeds—lives on in memory. Forgiveness is an unnatural act, and my wife was protesting its blatant unfairness.

A story from Genesis captures much the same sentiment. When I was a child listening to the story in Sunday
school, I could not understand the loops and twists in
the account of Joseph's reconciliation with his brothers. One moment Joseph acted harshly, throwing his
brothers in jail; the next moment he seemed overcome
with sorrow, leaving the room to blubber like a drunk.
He played tricks on his brothers, hiding money in their
grain sacks, seizing one as a hostage, accusing another
of stealing his silver cup. For months, maybe years, these
intrigues dragged on until finally Joseph could restrain
himself no longer. He summoned his brothers and dra-
matically forgave them.

I now see that story as a realistic depiction of the
unnatural act of forgiveness. The brothers Joseph
struggled to forgive were the very ones who had bullied
him, had cooked up schemes to murder him, had sold him
into slavery. Because of them he had spent the best years
of his youth moldering in an Egyptian dungeon. Though
he went on to triumph over adversity and though with
all his heart he now wanted to forgive these brothers, he
could not bring himself to that point, not yet. The wound
still hurt too much.

I view Genesis 42 – 45 as Joseph's way of saying, "I
think it's pretty amazing that I forgive you for the dastardly things you've done!" When grace finally broke
through to Joseph, the sound of his grief and love ech-
oed throughout the palace. *What is that wail? Is the king's*

minister sick? No, Joseph's health was fine. It was the sound of a man forgiving.

Behind every act of forgiveness lies a wound of betrayal, and the pain of being betrayed does not easily fade away. Leo Tolstoy thought he was getting his marriage off on the right foot when he asked his teenage fiancée to read his diaries, which spelled out in lurid detail all of his sexual dalliances. He wanted to keep no secrets from Sonya, to begin marriage with a clean slate, forgiven. Instead, Tolstoy's confession sowed the seeds for a marriage that would be held together by vines of hatred, not love.

"When he kisses me I'm always thinking, 'I'm not the first woman he has loved,'" wrote Sonya Tolstoy in her own diary. Some of his adolescent flings she could forgive, but not his affair with Axinya, a peasant woman who continued to work on the Tolstoy estate.

"One of these days I shall kill myself with jealousy," Sonya wrote after seeing the three-year-old son of the peasant woman, the spitting image of her husband. "If I could kill him [Tolstoy] and create a new person exactly the same as he is now, I would do so happily."

Another diary entry dates from January 14, 1909. "He relishes that peasant wench with her strong female body and her sunburnt legs, she allures him just as powerfully now as she did all those years ago ..." Sonya wrote those words when Axinya was a shriveled crone of eighty. For half a century jealousy and unforgiveness had blinded her, in the process destroying all love for her husband.

Against such malignant power, what chance stands the Christian response? Forgiveness is an unnatural act— Sonya Tolstoy, Joseph, and my wife express this truth as if by instinct.

I and the public know / What all school children learn, / Those to whom evil is done / Do evil in return.

W. H. Auden, who wrote those lines, understood that the law of nature admits no forgiveness. Do squirrels forgive cats for chasing them up trees or dolphins forgive sharks for eating their playmates? It's a dog-eat-dog world out there, not dog-forgive-dog. As for the human species, our major institutions—financial, political, even athletic—run on the same unrelenting principle. A baseball umpire never announces, "You were really out, but because of your exemplary spirit I'll call you safe." Or what nation responds to its belligerent neighbors with the proclamation, "You are right, we violated your borders. Will you please forgive us?"

The very taste of forgiveness seems somehow wrong. Even when we have committed a wrong, we want to earn our way back into the injured party's good graces. We prefer to crawl on our knees, to wallow, to do penance, to kill a lamb—and religion often obliges us. When the Holy Roman Emperor Henry IV decided to seek the pardon of Pope Gregory VII in 1077, he stood barefoot for three days in the snow outside the papal quarters in Italy. Probably,

Henry went away with a self-satisfied feeling, wearing frostbite scars as the stigmata of forgiveness.

"Despite a hundred sermons on forgiveness, we do not forgive easily, nor find ourselves easily forgiven. Forgiveness, we discover, is always harder than the sermons make it out to be," writes Elizabeth O'Connor. We nurse sores, go to elaborate lengths to rationalize our behavior, perpetuate family feuds, punish ourselves, punish others—all to avoid this most unnatural act.

On a visit to Bath, England, I saw a more natural response to being wronged. In the Roman ruins there, archeologists have uncovered various "curses" written in Latin and inscribed on tin or bronze placards. Centuries ago, users of the baths tossed in these prayers as an offering to the gods of the bath, much as moderns toss coins into fountains for good luck. One asked for a goddess's help in blood vengeance against whoever stole his six coins. Another read, "Docimedes has lost two gloves. He asks that the person who has stolen them should lose his mind and his eyes in the temple where she appoints."

As I looked at the Latin inscriptions and read their translations, it struck me that these prayers made good sense. Why not employ divine power to assist us with human justice here on earth? Many of the Psalms express the same sentiment, imploring God to help avenge some wrong. "Lord, if you can't make me thin, then make my friends look fat," humorist Erma Bombeck once prayed. What could be more human?

Instead, in a stunning reversal, Jesus instructed us to pray, "Forgive us our trespasses, as we forgive those who trespass against us." At the center of the Lord's Prayer, which Jesus taught us to recite, lurks the unnatural act of forgiveness. Roman bathers urged their gods to abet human justice; Jesus hinged God's forgiveness on our willingness to forgive unjust acts.

Charles Williams has said of the Lord's Prayer, "No word in English carries a greater possibility of terror than the little word 'as' in that clause." What makes the "as" so terrifying? The fact that Jesus plainly links our forgiven-ness by the Father with our forgiving-ness of fellow human beings. Jesus' next remark could not be more explicit: "If you do not forgive men their sins, your Father will not forgive your sins." Grace put to the test indeed.

It is one thing to get caught up in a cycle of ungrace with a spouse or business partner, and another thing entirely to get caught in such a cycle with Almighty God. Yet the Lord's Prayer pulls those two together: As we can allow ourselves to let go, to break the cycle, to start over, God can allow himself to let go, break the cycle, start over.

John Dryden wrote of the sobering effect of this truth. "More libels have been written against me, than almost any man now living," he protested, and prepared to lash out against his enemies. But "this consideration has often made me tremble when I was saying our Saviour's prayer;

for the plain condition of the forgiveness which we beg is the pardoning of others the offences which they have done to us; for which reason I have many times avoided the commission of that fault, even when I have been notoriously provoked."

Dryden was right to tremble. In a world that runs by the laws of ungrace, Jesus requires—no, demands—a response of forgiveness. So urgent is the need for forgiveness that it takes precedence over "religious" duties: "Therefore, if you are offering your gift at the altar and there remember that your brother has something against you, leave your gift there in front of the altar. First go and be reconciled to your brother; then come and offer your gift."

Jesus concluded his parable of the unforgiving servant with a scene of the master turning over the servant to jailers to be tortured. "This is how my heavenly Father will treat each of you unless you forgive your brother from your heart," Jesus said. I fervently wish these words were not in the Bible, but there they are, from the lips of Christ himself. God has granted us a terrible agency: by denying forgiveness to others, we are in effect determining them unworthy of God's forgiveness, and thus so are we. In some mysterious way, divine forgiveness depends on us.

Shakespeare put it succinctly in *Merchant of Venice*: "How shalt thou hope for mercy, rendering none?"

The author and speaker Tony Campolo sometimes asks students at secular universities what they know about Jesus. Can they recall anything Jesus said? By clear consensus they reply, "Love your enemies." More than any other teaching of Christ, that one stands out to an unbeliever. Such an attitude is unnatural, perhaps downright suicidal. It's hard enough to forgive your rotten brothers, as Joseph did, but your enemies? The gang of thugs down the block? Iranians? The drug dealers poisoning our nation?

Most ethicists would agree instead with the philosopher Immanuel Kant, who argued that a person should be forgiven only if he deserves it. But the very word *forgive* contains the word "give" (just as the word *pardon* contains *donum*, or gift). Like grace, forgiveness has about it the maddening quality of being undeserved, unmerited, unfair.

Why would God require of us an unnatural act that defies every primal instinct? What makes forgiveness so important that it becomes central to our faith? From my experience as an often-forgiven, sometimes-forgiving person, I can suggest several reasons. The first is theological.

Theologically, the Gospels give a straightforward answer to why God asks us to forgive: because that is what God is like. When Jesus first gave the command, "Love your enemies," he added this rationale: "... that you may be sons of your Father in heaven. He causes his sun to rise on the evil and the good, and sends rain on the righteous and the unrighteous."

Anyone, said Jesus, can love friends and family: "Do not even pagans do that?" Sons and daughters of the Father are called to a higher law, in order to resemble the forgiving Father. We are called to be like God, to bear God's family likeness.

Wrestling with the command to "love your enemies" while being persecuted under Nazi Germany, Dietrich Bonhoeffer finally concluded that it was this very quality of the "peculiar ... the extraordinary, the unusual" that sets a Christian apart from others. Even as he worked to undermine the regime, he followed Jesus' command to "Pray for those who persecute you." Bonhoeffer wrote,

> Through the medium of prayer we go to our enemy, stand by his side, and plead for him to God. Jesus does not promise that when we bless our enemies and do good to them they will not despitefully use and persecute us. They certainly will. But not even that can hurt or overcome us, so long as we pray for them.... We are doing vicariously for them what they cannot do for themselves.

Why did Bonhoeffer strive to love his enemies and pray for his persecutors? He had only one answer: "God loves his enemies—that is the glory of his love, as every follower of Jesus knows." If God forgave our debts, how can we not do the same?

Again the parable of the unforgiving servant comes to mind. The servant had every right to resent the few dollars his colleague owed him. By the laws of Roman justice, he had the right to throw the colleague into prison. Jesus did not dispute the servant's personal loss but, rather, set that loss against a master [God] who had already forgiven the servant several million dollars. Only the experience of being forgiven makes it possible for us to forgive.

I had a friend (now dead) who worked on the staff of Wheaton College for many years, during the course of which he heard several thousand chapel messages. In time most of these faded into a forgettable blur, but a few stood out. In particular he loved retelling the story of Sam Moffat, a professor at Princeton Seminary who had served as a missionary in China. Moffat told the Wheaton students a gripping tale of his flight from Communist pursuers. They seized his house and all his possessions, burned the missionary compound, and killed some of his closest friends. Moffat's own family barely escaped. When he left China, Moffat took with him a deep resentment against the followers of Chairman Mao, a resentment that metastasized inside him. Finally, he told the Wheaton students, he faced a singular crisis of faith. "I realized," said Moffat, "that if I have no forgiveness for the Communists, then I have no message at all."

The gospel of grace begins and ends with forgiveness. And people write songs with titles like "Amazing Grace" for one reason: grace is the only force in the universe powerful enough to break the chains that enslave generations. Grace alone melts ungrace.

One weekend I sat with ten Jews, ten Christians, and ten Muslims in a kind of encounter group led by author and psychiatrist M. Scott Peck, who hoped the weekend might lead to some sort of community, or at least the beginnings of reconciliation on a small scale. It did not. Fistfights almost broke out among these educated, sophisticated people. The Jews talked about all the horrible things done to them by Christians. The Muslims talked about all the horrible things done to them by Jews. We Christians tried to talk about our own problems, but they paled in contrast to stories of the Holocaust and the plight of Palestinian refugees, and so mainly we sat on the sidelines and listened to the other two groups recount the injustices of history.

At one point an articulate Jewish woman, who had been active in prior attempts at reconciliation with Arabs, turned to the Christians and said, "I believe we Jews have a lot to learn from you Christians about forgiveness. I see no other way around some of the logjams. And yet it seems so unfair, to forgive injustice. I am caught between forgiveness and justice."

I thought back to that weekend when I came across these words from Helmut Thielicke, a German who lived through the horrors of Nazism:

> This business of forgiving is by no means a simple thing.... We say, "Very well, if the other fellow is sorry and begs my pardon, I will forgive him, then I'll give in." We make of forgiveness a law of reciprocity. And this never works. For then both of us say to ourselves, "The other fellow has to make the first move." And then I watch like a hawk to see whether the other person will flash a signal to me with his eyes or whether I can detect some small hint between the lines of his letter which shows that he is sorry. I am always on the point of forgiving ... but I never forgive. I am far too just.

The only remedy, Thielicke concluded, was his realization that God had forgiven his sins and given him another chance—the lesson of the parable of the unforgiving servant. Breaking the cycle of ungrace means *taking the initiative*. Instead of waiting for his neighbor to make the first move, Thielicke must do so, defying the natural law of retribution and fairness. He did this only when he realized that God's initiative lay at the heart of the gospel he had been preaching but not practicing.

At the center of Jesus' parables of grace stands a God who takes the initiative toward us: a lovesick father who runs to meet the prodigal, a king who cancels a debt too large for any servant to reimburse, an employer who pays eleventh-hour workers the same as the first-hour crew, a banquet-giver who goes out to the highways and byways in search of undeserving guests.

God shattered the inexorable law of sin and retribution by invading earth, absorbing the worst we had to offer, crucifixion, and then fashioning from that cruel deed the remedy for the human condition. Calvary broke up the logjam between justice and forgiveness. By accepting onto his innocent self all the severe demands of justice, Jesus broke forever the chain of ungrace.

Like Helmut Thielicke, all too often I drift back into a tit-for-tat struggle that slams the door on forgiveness. *Why should I make the first move? I was the one wronged.* So I make no move, and cracks in the relationship appear, then widen. In time a chasm yawns open that seems impossible to cross. I feel sad, but seldom do I accept the blame. Instead, I justify myself and point out the small gestures I made toward reconciliation. I keep a mental accounting of those attempts so as to defend myself if I am ever blamed for the rift. I flee from the risk of grace to the security of ungrace.

Henri Nouwen, who defines forgiveness as "love practiced among people who love poorly," describes the process at work:

I have often said, "I forgive you," but even as I said these words my heart remained angry or resentful. I still wanted to hear the story that tells me that I was right after all; I still wanted to hear apologies and excuses; I still wanted the satisfaction of receiving some praise in return—if only the praise for being so forgiving!

But God's forgiveness is unconditional; it comes from a heart that does not demand anything for itself, a heart that is completely empty of self-seeking. It is this divine forgiveness that I have to practice in my daily life. It calls me to keep stepping over all my arguments that say forgiveness is unwise, unhealthy, and impractical. It challenges me to step over all my needs for gratitude and compliments. Finally, it demands of me that I step over that wounded part of my heart that feels hurt and wronged and that wants to stay in control and put a few conditions between me and the one whom I am asked to forgive.

One day I discovered this admonition from the apostle Paul tucked in among many other admonitions in Romans 12. Hate evil, Be joyful, Live in harmony, Do not be conceited—the list goes on and on. Then appears this verse, "Do not take revenge, my friends, but leave room for God's wrath, for it is written: 'It is mine to avenge; I will repay,' says the Lord."

At last I understood: in the final analysis, forgiveness is an act of faith. By forgiving another, I am trusting that God is a better justice-maker than I am. By forgiving, I release my own right to get even and leave all issues of fairness for God to work out. I leave in God's hands the scales that must balance justice and mercy.

When Joseph finally came to the place of forgiving his brothers, the hurt did not disappear, but the burden of being their judge fell away. Though wrong does not disappear when I forgive, it loses its grip on me and is taken over by God, who knows what to do. Such a decision involves risk, of course: the risk that God may not deal with the person as I would want. (The prophet Jonah, for instance, resented God for being more merciful than the Ninevites deserved.)

I never find forgiveness easy, and rarely do I find it completely satisfying. Nagging injustices remain, and the wounds still cause pain. I have to approach God again and again, yielding to him the residue of what I thought I had committed to him long ago. I do so because the Gospels make clear the connection: God forgives my debts as I forgive my debtors. The reverse is also true: Only by living in the stream of God's grace will I find the strength to respond with grace toward others.

A cease-fire between human beings depends upon a cease-fire with God.

Chapter 6

WHY FORGIVE?

I participated in a lively discussion on the topic of forgiveness the week Jeffrey Dahmer died in prison. Dahmer, a mass murderer, had abused and then killed seventeen young men, cannibalizing them and storing body parts in his refrigerator. His arrest caused a shake-up in the Milwaukee police department when it became known that officers had ignored the desperate pleas of a Vietnamese teenager who tried to escape by running, naked and bleeding, from Dahmer's apartment. That boy too became Dahmer's victim, one of eleven corpses found in his apartment.

In November of 1994, Dahmer himself was murdered, beaten to death with a broom handle wielded by a fellow prisoner. Television news reports that day included interviews with the grieving relatives of Dahmer's victims, most of whom said they regretted Dahmer's murder only because it ended his life too soon. He should have had to suffer by being forced to live longer and think about the terrible things he had done.

One network showed a television program taped a few weeks before Dahmer's death. The interviewer asked him how he could possibly do the things he had been convicted of. At the time he didn't believe in God, Dahmer said, and so he felt accountable to no one. He began with petty crimes, experimented with small acts of cruelty, and then just kept going, further and further. Nothing restrained him.

Dahmer then told of his recent religious conversion. He had been baptized in the prison whirlpool and was spending all his time reading religious material given him by a local Church of Christ minister. The camera switched to an interview with the prison chaplain, who affirmed that Dahmer had indeed repented and was now one of his most faithful worshipers.

The discussion in my small group tended to divide between those who had watched only the news programs on Dahmer's death and those who had also watched the interview with Dahmer. The former group saw Dahmer as a monster, and any reports of a jailhouse conversion they dismissed out-of-hand. The relatives' anguished faces had made a deep impression. One person said candidly, "Crimes that bad can never be forgiven. He couldn't be sincere."

Those who had seen the interview with Dahmer were not so sure. They agreed his crimes were heinous beyond belief. Yet he had seemed contrite, even humble.

The conversation turned to the question, "Is anyone ever beyond forgiveness?" No one left the evening feeling entirely comfortable with the answers.

The scandal of forgiveness confronts anyone who agrees to a moral cease-fire just because someone says, "I'm sorry." When I feel wronged, I can contrive a hundred reasons against forgiveness. *He needs to learn a lesson. I don't want to encourage irresponsible behavior. I'll let her stew for a while; it will do her good. She needs to learn that actions have consequences. I was the wronged party—it's not up to me to make the first move. How can I forgive if he's not even sorry?* I marshal my arguments until something happens to wear down my resistance. When I finally soften to the point of granting forgiveness, it seems a capitulation, a leap from hard logic to mushy sentiment.

Why do I ever make such a leap? I have already mentioned one factor that motivates me as a Christian: I am commanded to, as the child of a Father who forgives. But Christians have no monopoly on forgiveness. Why do any of us, Christian or unbeliever alike, choose this unnatural act? I can identify at least three pragmatic reasons, and the more I ponder these reasons for forgiveness, the more I recognize in them a logic that seems not only "hard" but foundational.

First, forgiveness alone can halt the cycle of blame and pain, breaking the chain of ungrace. In the New

Testament the most common Greek word for forgiveness means, literally, to release, to hurl away, to free yourself.

I readily admit that forgiveness is unfair. Hinduism, with its doctrine of *karma*, provides a far more satisfying sense of fairness. Hindu scholars have calculated with mathematical precision how long it may take for one person's justice to work itself out: for punishment to balance out all my wrongs in this life and future lives, 6,800,000 incarnations should suffice.

Marriage gives a glimpse of the karma process at work. Two stubborn people live together, get on each other's nerves, and perpetuate the power struggle through an emotional tug-of-war. "I can't believe you forgot your own mother's birthday," says one.

"Wait a minute, aren't you supposed to be in charge of the calendar?"

"Don't try to pass the blame to me—she's your mother."

"Yes, but I told you just last week to remind me. Why didn't you?"

"You're crazy—it's your own mother. Can't you keep track of your own mother's birthday?"

"Why should I? It's your job to remind me."

The inane dialogue bleats on and on through, say, 6,800,000 cycles until at last one of the partners says, "Stop! I'll break the chain." And the only way to do so is forgiveness: *I'm sorry. Will you forgive me?*

The word *resentment* expresses what happens if

the cycle goes uninterrupted. It means, literally, "to feel again": resentment clings to the past, relives it over and over, picks each fresh scab so that the wound never heals. This pattern doubtless began with the very first couple on earth. "Think of all the squabbles Adam and Eve must have had in the course of their nine hundred years," wrote Martin Luther. "Eve would say, 'You ate the apple,' and Adam would retort, 'You gave it to me.'"

Two novels by Nobel laureates illustrate the pattern in a modern setting. In *Love in the Time of Cholera*, Gabriel García Márquez portrays a marriage that disintegrates over a bar of soap. It was the wife's job to keep the house in order, including provision of towels, toilet paper, and soap in the bathroom. One day she forgot to replace the soap, an oversight that her husband mentioned in an exaggerated way ("I've been bathing for almost a week without any soap"), and that she vigorously denied. Although it turned out that she had indeed forgotten, her pride was at stake and she would not back down. For the next seven months they slept in separate rooms and ate in silence.

"Even when they were old and placid," writes Márquez, "they were very careful about bringing it up, for the barely healed wounds could begin to bleed again as if they had been inflicted only yesterday." How can a bar of soap ruin a marriage? Because neither partner would say, "Stop. This cannot go on. I'm sorry. Forgive me."

The Knot of Vipers by François Mauriac tells a similar story of an old man who spends the last decades—decades!—of his marriage sleeping down the hall from his wife. A rift had opened thirty years before over whether the husband showed enough concern when their five-year-old daughter fell ill. Now, neither husband nor wife is willing to take the first step. Every night he waits for her to approach him, but she never appears. Every night she lies awake waiting for him to approach her, and he never appears. Neither will break the cycle that began years before. Neither will forgive.

In her memoir of a truly dysfunctional family, *The Liars' Club*, Mary Karr tells of a Texas uncle who remained married to his wife but did not speak to her for forty years after a fight over how much money she spent on sugar. One day he took out a lumber saw and sawed their house exactly in half. He nailed up planks to cover the raw sides and moved one of the halves behind a copse of scruffy pine trees on the same acre of ground. There the two, husband and wife, lived out the rest of their days in separate half-houses.

Forgiveness offers a way out. It does not settle all questions of blame and fairness—often it pointedly evades those questions—but it does allow a relationship to start over, to begin anew. In that way, said Solzhenitsyn, we differ from all animals. Not our capacity to think, but our capacity to repent and to forgive makes us different. Only humans can perform that most unnatural act, which transcends the relentless law of nature.

If we do not transcend nature, we remain bound to

the people we cannot forgive, held in their vise grip. This principle applies even when one party is wholly innocent and the other wholly to blame, for the innocent party will bear the wound until he or she can find a way to release it—and forgiveness is the only way. Oscar Hijuelos wrote a poignant novel, *Mr. Ives' Christmas*, about a man who is throttled by bitterness until somehow he finds it within himself to forgive the Latino criminal who murdered his son. Although Ives himself did nothing wrong, for decades the murder has kept him an emotional prisoner.

Sometimes I let my mind wander and imagine a world with no forgiveness. What would happen if every child bore grudges against his or her parents, and every family passed down feuds to future generations? I told of one family—Daisy, Margaret, Michael—and the virus of ungrace that afflicts them all. I know, respect, and enjoy each member of that family, separately. Yet even though they share almost the same genetic code, today they cannot sit in the same room together. All of them have protested to me their innocence—but innocents too suffer the results of ungrace. "I never want to see you again as long as I live!" Margaret yelled at her son. She got her wish, and now she suffers from it every day. I can see the pain in the narrowing of her eyes and the tensing of her jaw every time I say the word, "Michael."

I let my imagination run further, to a world in which every former colony harbors grudges against its former imperial power, and every race hates every other race, and every tribe battles its rivals as if all of history's grievances amass behind every contact of nation, race, and tribe. I get depressed when I imagine such a scene because it seems so close to history as it now exists. As the Jewish philosopher Hannah Arendt said, the only remedy for the inevitability of history is forgiveness; otherwise, we remain trapped in the "predicament of irreversibility."

Not to forgive imprisons me in the past and locks out all potential for change. I thus yield control to another, my enemy, and doom myself to suffer the consequences of the wrong. I once heard an immigrant rabbi make an astonishing statement. "Before coming to America, I had to forgive Adolf Hitler," he said. "I did not want to bring Hitler inside me to my new country."

We forgive not merely to fulfill some higher law of morality; we do it for ourselves. As Lewis Smedes points out, "The first and often the only person to be healed by forgiveness is the person who does the forgiveness.... When we genuinely forgive, we set a prisoner free and then discover that the prisoner we set free was us."

For the biblical Joseph, who had borne a well-deserved grudge against his brothers, forgiveness spilled out in the form of tears and groans. These, like childbirth's, were harbingers of liberation, and through them Joseph gained at last his freedom. He named his son Manasseh, "one who causes to be forgotten."

The only thing harder than forgiveness is the alternative.

The second great power of forgiveness is that it can loosen the stranglehold of guilt in the perpetrator.

Guilt does its corrosive work even when consciously repressed. In 1993 a Ku Klux Klansman named Henry Alexander made a confession to his wife. In 1957 he and several other Klansmen had pulled an African-American truck driver from his cab, marched him to a deserted bridge high above a swift river, and made him jump, screaming, to his death. Alexander was charged with the crime in 1976—it took nearly twenty years to bring him to trial—pled innocent and was acquitted by a white jury. For thirty-six years he insisted on his innocence, until the day in 1993 when he confessed the truth to his wife. "I don't even know what God has planned for me. I don't even know how to pray for myself," he told her. A few days later, he died.

Alexander's wife wrote a letter of apology to the truck driver's widow, a letter subsequently printed in *The New York Times*. "Henry lived a lie all his life, and he made me live it too," she wrote. For all those years she had believed her husband's protestations of innocence. He showed no outward sign of remorse until the last days of his life, too late to attempt public restitution. Yet he could not carry the terrible secret of guilt to his grave. After thirty-six years of fierce denial, he still needed the release only forgiveness could provide.

Another member of the Ku Klux Klan, the Grand Dragon Larry Trapp of Lincoln, Nebraska, made national headlines in 1992 when he renounced his hatred, tore down his Nazi flags, and destroyed his many cartons of hate literature. As Kathryn Watterson recounts in the book *Not by the Sword*, Trapp had been won over by the forgiving love of a Jewish cantor and his family. Though Trapp had sent them vile pamphlets mocking big-nosed Jews and denying the Holocaust, though he had threatened violence in phone calls made to their home, though he had targeted their synagogue for bombing, the cantor's family consistently responded with compassion and concern. Diabetic since childhood, Trapp was confined to a wheelchair and rapidly going blind; the cantor's family invited Trapp into their home to care for him. "They showed me such love that I couldn't help but love them back," Trapp later said. He spent his last months of life seeking forgiveness from Jewish groups, the NAACP, and the many individuals he had hated.

In recent years audiences worldwide have watched a drama of forgiveness played out onstage in the musical version of *Les Misérables*. The musical follows its original source, Victor Hugo's sprawling novel, in telling the story of Jean Valjean, a French prisoner hounded and ultimately transformed by forgiveness.

Sentenced to a nineteen-year term of hard labor for the crime of stealing bread, Jean Valjean gradually hardened into a tough convict. No one could beat him in a fistfight. No one could break his will. At last Valjean earned his release. Convicts in those days had to carry identity cards, however, and no innkeeper would let a dangerous felon spend the night. For four days he wandered the village roads, seeking shelter against the weather, until finally a kindly bishop had mercy on him.

That night Jean Valjean lay still in an overcomfortable bed until the bishop and his sister drifted off to sleep. He rose from his bed, rummaged through the cupboard for the family silver, and crept off into the darkness.

The next morning three policemen knocked on the bishop's door, with Valjean in tow. They had caught the convict in flight with the purloined silver, and were ready to put the scoundrel in chains for life.

The bishop responded in a way that no one, especially Jean Valjean, expected.

"So here you are!" he cried to Valjean. "I'm delighted to see you. Had you forgotten that I gave you the candlesticks as well? They're silver like the rest, and worth a good 200 francs. Did you forget to take them?"

Jean Valjean's eyes had widened. He was now staring at the old man with an expression no words can convey.

Valjean was no thief, the bishop assured the gendarmes. "This silver was my gift to him."

When the gendarmes withdrew, the bishop gave the candlesticks to his guest, now speechless and trembling.

"Do not forget, do not ever forget," said the bishop, "that you have promised me to use the money to make yourself an honest man."

The power of the bishop's act, defying every human instinct for revenge, changed Jean Valjean's life forever. A naked encounter with forgiveness—especially since he had never repented—melted the granite defenses of his soul. He kept the candlesticks as a precious memento of grace and dedicated himself from then on to helping others in need.

Hugo's novel stands, in fact, as a two-edged parable of forgiveness. A detective named Javert, who knows no law but justice, stalks Jean Valjean mercilessly over the next two decades. As Valjean is transformed by forgiveness, the detective is consumed by a thirst for retribution. When Valjean saves Javert's life—the prey showing grace to his pursuer—the detective senses his black-and-white world beginning to crumble. Unable to cope with a grace that goes against all instinct, and finding within himself no corresponding forgiveness, Javert jumps off a bridge into the Seine River.

Scandalous forgiveness, such as that offered Valjean by the bishop, allows the possibility of transformation in the guilty party. Lewis Smedes details this process of "spiritual surgery":

> When you forgive someone, you slice away the wrong from the person who did it. You disengage that person from his hurtful act. You recreate

him. At one moment you identify him ineradicably as the person who did you wrong. The next moment you change that identity. He is remade in your memory.

You think of him now not as the person who hurt you, but a person who needs you. You feel him now not as the person who alienated you, but as the person who belongs to you. Once you branded him as a person powerful in evil, but now you see him as a person weak in his needs. You recreated your past by recreating the person whose wrong made your past painful.

Smedes adds many cautions. Forgiveness is not the same as pardon, he advises: you may forgive one who wronged you and still insist on a just punishment for that wrong. If you can bring yourself to the point of forgiveness, though, you will release its healing power both in you and in the person who wronged you.

A friend of mine who works in the inner city questions whether forgiveness of those who have not repented makes sense. This man daily sees the results of evil from child abuse, drugs, violence, and prostitution. "If I know something is wrong and 'forgive' without addressing the wrong, what am I doing?" he asks. "I am potentially enabling rather than freeing."

My friend has told me stories of the people he works with, and I agree that some of them seem beyond the pale of forgiveness. Yet I cannot forget the stirring scene of the bishop forgiving Jean Valjean, who had admitted no wrong. Forgiveness has its own extraordinary power which reaches beyond law and beyond justice. Before *Les Misérables* I read *The Count of Monte Cristo*, a novel by Hugo's compatriot Alexandre Dumas, which tells the story of a wronged man working exquisite revenge on the four men who had framed him. Dumas's novel appealed to my sense of justice; Hugo's awakened in me a sense of grace.

Justice has a good and righteous and rational kind of power. The power of grace is different: unworldly, transforming, supernatural. Reginald Denny, the truck driver assaulted during the riots in South Central Los Angeles, demonstrated this power of grace. The entire nation watched the helicopter video of two men smashing his truck window with a brick, hauling him from a cab, then beating him with a broken bottle and kicking him until the side of his face caved in. In court, his tormentors were belligerent and unrepentant, yielding no ground. With worldwide media looking on, Reginald Denny, his face still swollen and misshapen, shook off the protests of his lawyers, made his way over to the mothers of the two defendants, hugged them, and told them he forgave them. The mothers embraced Denny, one declaring, "I love you."

I do not know what effect that scene had on the surly defendants, sitting in handcuffs not far away. But I do know that forgiveness, and only forgiveness, can begin the thaw in the guilty party. And I also know what effect it has on me when a fellow worker, or my wife, comes to me without prompting and offers forgiveness for some wrong I am too proud and stubborn to confess.

Forgiveness—undeserved, unearned—can cut the cords and let the oppressive burden of guilt roll away. The New Testament shows a resurrected Jesus leading Peter by the hand through a three-fold ritual of forgiveness. Peter need not go through life with the guilty, hangdog look of one who has betrayed the Son of God. Oh, no. On the backs of such transformed sinners Christ would build his church.

Forgiveness breaks the cycle of blame and loosens the stranglehold of guilt. It accomplishes these two things through a remarkable linkage, placing the forgiver on the same side as the party who did the wrong. Through it we realize we are not as different from the wrongdoer as we would like to think. "I also am other than what I imagine myself to be. To know this is forgiveness," said Simone Weil.

I mentioned a small group discussion on forgiveness revolving around the case of Jeffrey Dahmer. Like many such discussions, it kept drifting away from personal illustrations, toward the abstract and theoretical. We discussed other horrific crimes, and Bosnia, and the Holocaust. Almost by accident, the word "divorce" came up, and to our surprise Rebecca spoke up.

Rebecca is a quiet woman, and in weeks of meeting together she had rarely opened her mouth. At the mention of divorce, though, she proceeded to tell her own story. She had married a pastor who had some renown as a retreat leader. It became apparent, however, that her husband had a dark side. He dabbled in pornography, and on his trips to other cities he solicited prostitutes. Sometimes he asked Rebecca for forgiveness, sometimes he did not. In time, he left her for another woman, Julianne.

Rebecca told us how painful it was for her, a pastor's wife, to suffer this humiliation. Some church members who had respected her husband treated her as if his sexual straying had been her fault. Devastated, she found herself pulling away from human contact, unable to trust another person. She could never put her husband out of mind because they had children and she had to make regular contact with him in order to arrange his visitation privileges.

Rebecca had the increasing sense that unless she forgave her former husband, a hard lump of revenge would be passed on to their children. For months she prayed. At first her prayers seemed as vengeful as some of the Psalms: she asked God to give her ex-husband "what he deserved." Finally she came to the place of letting God, not herself, determine "what he deserved."

One night Rebecca called her ex-husband and said, in a shaky, strained voice, "I want you to know that I forgive you for what you've done to me. And I forgive Julianne too." He laughed off her apology, unwilling to admit he had done anything wrong. Despite his rebuff, that conversation helped Rebecca get past her bitter feelings.

A few years later Rebecca got a hysterical phone call from Julianne, the woman who had "stolen" her husband. She had been attending a ministerial conference with him in Minneapolis, and he had left the hotel room to go for a walk. A few hours passed, then Julianne heard from the police: her husband had been picked up for soliciting a prostitute.

On the phone with Rebecca, Julianne was sobbing. "I never believed you," she said. "I kept telling myself that even if what you said was true, he had changed. And now this. I feel so ashamed, and hurt, and guilty. I have no one on earth who can understand. Then I remembered the night when you said you forgave us. I thought maybe you could understand what I'm going through. It's a terrible thing to ask, I know, but could I come talk to you?"

Somehow Rebecca found the courage to invite Julianne over that same evening. They sat in her living room, cried together, shared stories of betrayal, and in the end prayed together. Julianne now points to that night as the time when she became a Christian.

Our group was hushed as Rebecca told her story. She was describing forgiveness not in the abstract, but in a nearly incomprehensible scene of human linkage: husband-stealer and abandoned wife kneeling side by side on a living-room floor, praying.

"For a long time, I had felt foolish about forgiving my husband," Rebecca told us. "But that night I realized the fruit of forgiveness. Julianne was right. I could understand what she was going through. And because I had been there too, I could be on her side, instead of her enemy. We both had been betrayed by the same man. Now it was up to me to teach her how to overcome the hatred and revenge and guilt she was feeling."

In *The Art of Forgiving*, Lewis Smedes makes the striking observation that the Bible portrays God going through progressive stages when he forgives, much as we humans do. First, God rediscovers the humanity of the person who wronged him, by removing the barrier created by sin. Second, God surrenders his right to get even, choosing instead to bear the cost in his own body. Finally, God revises his feelings toward us, finding a way to "justify" us so that when he looks upon us he sees his own adopted children, with his divine image restored.

It occurred to me, as I thought about Smedes's insights, that the gracious miracle of God's forgiveness was made possible because of the linkage that occurred when God came to earth in Christ. Somehow God had to come to terms with these creatures he desperately wanted to love—but how? Experientially, God did not know what it was like to be tempted to sin, to have a trying day. On earth, living among us, he learned what it was like. He put himself on our side.

The book of Hebrews makes explicit this mystery of incarnation: "We do not have a high priest who is unable to sympathize with our weaknesses, but we have one who has been tempted in every way, just as we are—yet was without sin." Second Corinthians goes even further: "God made him who had no sin to be sin for us." You cannot get any more explicit than that. God bridged the gap; he took our side all the way. And because he did, Hebrews affirms, Jesus can present our case to the Father. He has been here. He understands.

From the Gospels' accounts, it seems forgiveness was not easy for God, either. "If it is possible, may this cup be taken from me," Jesus prayed, contemplating the cost, and the sweat rolled off him like drops of blood. There was no other way. Finally, in one of his last statements before dying, he said, "Forgive them"—all of them, the Roman soldiers, the religious leaders, his disciples who had fled in darkness, you, me—"Forgive them, for they do not know what they are doing." Only by becoming a human being could the Son of God truly say, "They do not know what they are doing." Having lived among us, he now understood.

Chapter 7

GETTING EVEN

One day I picked up a book I had read several years before: *The Sunflower* by Simon Wiesenthal. It recounts a small incident that took place during this century's most successful "ethnic cleansing" campaign, an incident that does much to explain what propelled Wiesenthal to become the foremost hunter of Nazis and a relentless public voice against hate crimes. The book centers on forgiveness, and I turned to it for insight into what role forgiveness might play globally.

In 1944 Wiesenthal was a young Polish prisoner of the Nazis. He had looked on, helpless, as Nazi soldiers killed his grandmother on the stairway of her home and as they forced his mother into a freight car crammed with elderly Jewish women. Altogether, eighty-nine of his Jewish relatives would die at the hands of the Nazis. Wiesenthal himself tried without success to commit suicide when first captured.

One bright, sunny day as Wiesenthal's prison detail was cleaning rubbish out of a hospital for German casualties, a nurse approached him. "Are you a Jew?" she asked hesitantly, then signaled him to accompany her. Apprehensive, Wiesenthal followed her up a stairway and down a hallway until they reached a dark, musty room where a lone soldier lay swathed in bandages. White gauze covered the man's face, with openings cut out for mouth, nose, and ears.

The nurse disappeared, closing the door behind her to leave the young prisoner alone with the spectral figure. The wounded man was an SS officer, and he had summoned Wiesenthal for a deathbed confession. "My name is Karl," said a raspy voice that came from somewhere within the bandages. "I must tell you of this horrible deed—tell you because you are a Jew."

Karl began his story by reminiscing about his Catholic upbringing and his childhood faith, which he had lost while in the Hitler Youth Corps. He later volunteered for the SS and served with distinction and had only recently returned, badly wounded, from the Russian front.

Three times as Karl tried to tell his story, Wiesenthal pulled away as if to leave. Each time the officer reached out to grab his arm with a white, nearly bloodless hand. He begged him to listen to what he had just experienced in the Ukraine.

In the town of Dnyepropetrovsk, abandoned by the retreating Russians, Karl's unit stumbled onto booby traps that killed thirty of their soldiers. As an act of revenge, the SS rounded up three hundred Jews, herded them into a three-story house, doused it with gasoline, and fired grenades at it. Karl and his men encircled the house, their guns drawn to shoot anyone who tried to escape.

"The screams from the house were horrible," he said, reliving the moment. "I saw a man with a small child in his arms. His clothes were alight. By his side stood a woman, doubtless the mother of the child. With his free hand the man covered the child's eyes, then he jumped into the street. Seconds later the mother followed. Then from the other windows fell burning bodies. We shot … Oh God!"

All this time Simon Wiesenthal sat in silence, letting the German soldier speak. Karl went on to describe other atrocities, but he kept circling back to the scene of that young boy with black hair and dark eyes, falling from a building, target practice for the SS rifles. "I am left here with my guilt," he concluded at last:

> In the last hours of my life you are with me. I do not know who you are, I know only that you are a Jew and that is enough.
>
> I know that what I have told you is terrible. In the long nights while I have been waiting for death, time and time again I have longed to talk about it to a Jew and beg forgiveness from him. Only I didn't know whether there were any Jews

left ... I know what I am asking is almost too much for you, but without your answer I cannot die in peace.

Simon Wiesenthal, an architect in his early twenties, now a prisoner dressed in a shabby uniform marked with the yellow Star of David, felt the immense crushing burden of his race bear down on him. He stared out the window at the sunlit courtyard. He looked at the eyeless heap of bandages lying in the bed. He watched a bluebottle fly buzzing the dying man's body, attracted by the smell.

"At last I made up my mind," Wiesenthal writes, "and without a word I left the room."

The Sunflower takes forgiveness out of the theoretical and thrusts it in the midst of living history. I chose to reread the book because the dilemma Wiesenthal faced had so many parallels with moral dilemmas that are still tearing the world apart in places like Africa and the Middle East.

The first half of Wiesenthal's book tells the story I have just summarized. The next half records reactions to that story from such luminaries as Abraham Heschel, Martin Marty, Cynthia Ozick, Gabriel Marcel, Jacques Maritain, Herbert Marcuse, and Primo Levi. In the end, Wiesenthal turned to them for advice on whether he had done right.

The SS officer Karl soon died, unforgiven by a Jew,

but Simon Wiesenthal lived on to be liberated from a death camp by American troops. The scene in the hospital room haunted him like a ghost. After the war Wiesenthal visited the officer's mother in Stuttgart, hoping somehow to exorcise the memory of that day. Instead, the visit only made the officer more human, for the mother spoke tenderly of her son's pious youth. Wiesenthal could not bear to tell her how her son ended up.

Over the years, Wiesenthal asked many rabbis and priests what he should have done. Finally, more than twenty years after the war had ended, he wrote down the story and sent it to the brightest ethical minds he knew: Jew and Gentile, Catholic, Protestant, and irreligious. "What would you have done in my place?" he asked them.

Of the thirty-two men and women who responded, only six said that Wiesenthal had erred in not forgiving the German. Two Christians pointed to Wiesenthal's lingering discomfort as a twinge of conscience that could only be stilled by forgiveness. One of them, a black man who had served in the French Resistance, said, "I can understand your refusal to forgive. This is entirely in accordance with the spirit of the Bible, with the spirit of the Old Law. But there is the New Law, that of Christ as expressed in the Gospels. As a Christian, I think you should have forgiven."

A few others waffled, but most of the respondents agreed Simon Wiesenthal had done the right thing. What moral or legal authority had he to forgive crimes done to someone else? they asked. One writer quoted the poet Dryden, "Forgiveness, to the injured doth belong."

A few of the Jewish respondents said that the enormity of Nazi crimes had exceeded all possibility of forgiveness. Herbert Gold, an American author and professor, declared, "The guilt for this horror lies so heavily on the Germans of that time that no personal reaction to it is unjustifiable." Said another, "The millions of innocent people who were tortured and slaughtered would have to come back to life before I could forgive." Novelist Cynthia Ozick was fierce: "Let the SS man die unshriven. Let him go to hell." A Christian writer confessed, "I think I would strangle him in his bed."

A few commentators questioned the whole notion of forgiveness. One professor disdained forgiveness as an act of sensual pleasure, the sort of thing lovers do after a spat before climbing back into bed. It has no place, she said, in a world of genocide and Holocaust. Forgive, and the whole business might easily repeat itself.

When I first read *The Sunflower*, ten years before, I was taken aback by the near unanimity of the responses. I expected more of the Christian theologians to speak of mercy. But this time as I reread the eloquent replies to Wiesenthal's question I was struck by the terrible, crystalline logic of unforgiveness. In a world of unspeakable atrocity, forgiveness indeed seems unjust, unfair, irrational. Individuals and families must learn to forgive, yes, but how do such high-minded principles apply in a case like Nazi Germany? As the philosopher Herbert Marcuse put it, "One cannot, and should not go around happily killing and torturing and then, when the moment has come, simply ask, and receive, forgiveness."

Is it too much to expect that the high ethical ideals of the gospel—of which forgiveness lies at the core—might transpose into the brutal world of politics and international diplomacy? In such a world what chance stands something as ethereal as forgiveness? These questions nagged at me as I reread Wiesenthal's story while listening to the unremitting bad news from the world's conflict zones.

My Jewish friends have spoken with admiration of the Christian emphasis on forgiveness. I have presented it as our strongest weapon to disarm the counterforce of ungrace. And yet as the great Jewish scholar Joseph Klausner pointed out early in this century, the Christians' very insistence on such ideals leaves us vulnerable to a devastating critique. "The religion has stood for what is highest ethically and ideally," writes Klausner, "while the political and social life has remained at the other extreme of barbarity and paganism."

Klausner claims that the failures of Christian history prove his point that Jesus taught an impractical ethic that will not work in the real world. He mentions the Spanish Inquisition, which "was not thought to be incompatible with Christianity." A contemporary critic might add to his list Yugoslavia, Rwanda, and yes, even Nazi Germany, for all three of these conflicts took place in so-called Christian nations.

Does the Christian emphasis on love, grace, and forgiveness have any relevance outside quarreling families or church encounter groups? In a world where force matters most, a lofty ideal like forgiveness may seem as insubstantial as vapor. Stalin understood this principle all too well when he scoffed at the moral authority of the church: "How many divisions has the Pope?"

To be honest, I do not know how I would have responded in Simon Wiesenthal's place. Can we, should we forgive crimes of which we are not the victims? Karl the SS officer repented, making his case clearer, but what of the stony faces lined up, almost smirking, at the trials in Nuremberg and Stuttgart? Martin Marty, one of the Christian respondents in Wiesenthal's book, wrote these lines, with which I am tempted to agree: "I can only respond with silence. Non-Jews and perhaps especially Christians should not give advice about Holocaust experience to its heirs for the next two thousand years. And then we shall have nothing to say."

Still, I must admit that as I read the eloquent voices in support of unforgiveness, I could not help wondering which carries a higher cost, forgiveness or unforgiveness. Herbert Gold judged that "no personal reaction to it [German guilt] is unjustifiable." Oh? What about the revenge execution of all surviving Germans—would that be justifiable?

The strongest argument in favor of grace is the alternative, a world of ungrace. The strongest argument for forgiveness is the alternative, a permanent state of unforgiveness. I grant that the Holocaust creates special conditions. What of other, more contemporary examples? Where unforgiveness reigns, as essayist Lance Morrow has pointed out, a Newtonian law comes into play: For every atrocity there must be an equal and opposite atrocity.

The ethnic group known as Serbs are everybody's whipping boy for what happened to tear apart the former Yugoslavia. (Note the language used to describe them in *Time* magazine's supposedly objective news section: "What has happened in Bosnia is just squalor and barbarism—the filthy work of liars and cynics manipulating tribal prejudices, using atrocity propaganda and old blood feuds to accomplish the unclean political result of 'ethnic cleansing.'") Caught up in righteous—and wholly appropriate—revulsion over Serbian atrocities, the world overlooks one fact: the Serbs are simply following the terrible logic of unforgiveness.

Nazi Germany, the very same regime that eliminated eighty-nine members of Simon Wiesenthal's family and that provoked such harsh words from refined people like Cynthia Ozick and Herbert Marcuse, included the Serbs in their "ethnic cleansing" campaign during World War II. True, in the 1990s the Serbs killed tens of thousands—but during Nazi occupation of Balkan territory in the 1940s, the Germans and Croats killed hundreds of thousands of Serbs, Gypsies, and Jews. Historical memory lives on: in the late war German neo-Nazis enlisted to fight alongside the Croats, and units of the Croatian Army brazenly flew swastika flags and the old Croatian Fascist symbol.

"Never again," the rallying cry of Holocaust survivors, is also what inspired the Serbs to defy the United Nations and virtually the entire world. Never again will they let Croats rule over territory populated by Serbs. Never again will they let Muslims, either: the last war they fought with Muslims led to five centuries of Turkish rule (in historical perspective, a period more than twice as long as the United States has even existed).

In the logic of unforgiveness, not to strike against the enemy would betray ancestors and the sacrifices they made. There is one major flaw in the law of revenge, however: it never settles the score. The Turks got revenge in 1389, at the Battle of Kosovo; the Croats got it in the 1940s; now it's our turn, say the Serbs. Yet one day, as the Serbs surely know, the descendants of today's raped and mutilated victims will arise to seek vengeance on the avengers. The trapdoor has been opened, and wild bats flap about.

In the words of Lewis Smedes:

> Vengeance is a passion to get even. It is a hot desire to give back as much pain as someone gave you.... The problem with revenge is that it

never gets what it wants; it never evens the score. Fairness never comes. The chain reaction set off by every act of vengeance always takes its unhindered course. It ties both the injured and the injurer to an escalator of pain. Both are stuck on the escalator as long as parity is demanded, and the escalator never stops, never lets anyone off.

Forgiveness may be unfair—it is, by definition—but at least it provides a way to halt the juggernaut of retribution. Today, as I write, violence is either breaking out or smoldering just under the surface between China and Taiwan, India and Pakistan, Russia and Chechnya, Great Britain and Ireland, and especially between Jews and Arabs and Sunnis and Shiites in the Middle East. Each of these disputes traces back decades, centuries, or, in the case of the Jews and Arabs, millennia. Each side strives to overcome an injustice from the past, to right a perceived wrong.

Theologian Romano Guardini offers this diagnosis of the fatal flaw in the search for revenge: "As long as you are tangled in wrong and revenge, blow and counterblow, aggression and defense, you will be constantly drawn into fresh wrong.... Only forgiveness frees us from the injustice of others." If everyone followed the "eye for an eye" principle of justice, observed Gandhi, eventually the whole world would go blind.

We have many vivid demonstrations of the law of unforgiveness. In Shakespeare's and Sophocles' historical tragedies, bodies litter the stage. Macbeth, Richard III, Titus Andronicus, and Elektra must kill and kill and kill until they have their revenge, then live in fear lest some enemies have survived to seek counter-revenge.

Francis Ford Coppola's *Godfather* trilogy and Clint Eastwood's *Unforgiven* illustrate the same law. We see the law at work in IRA terrorists who blow up shoppers in downtown London in part because of atrocities committed back in 1649—which in turn were ordered by Oliver Cromwell to avenge a massacre in 1641. We see it in Sri Lanka and in Algeria and the Sudan and in the feuding republics of the former Soviet Union.

Simply acknowledge your crimes against us, say the Armenians to the Turks, and we'll stop blowing up airplanes and assassinating your diplomats. Turkey adamantly refuses. At one point during the Iran hostage crisis, the Iranian government announced they would release all hostages unharmed if the U.S. President apologized for past support of the Shah's oppressive regime. Jimmy Carter, a born-again Christian who understands forgiveness and has gained a deserved reputation as a peacemaker, declined. No apologies, he said. Our national honor was at stake.

I've found that a kind word with a gun gets more than a kind word," said John Dillinger. His observation helps explain why poor countries today spend up to half their annual income on weapons. In a fallen world, force works.

Helmut Thielicke recalls his first Bible study after becoming a pastor in the German state church. Determined to trust Jesus' saying "All power is given unto me in heaven and in earth," he tried to assure himself that even Adolf Hitler, then in power, was a mere puppet hanging by strings in the hands of a sovereign God. The group assembled for Bible study consisted of two elderly ladies and an even older, slightly palsied organist. Meanwhile, outside in the streets marched the spit-shine battalions of Hitler's Youth Corps. "The kingdom of heaven is like a grain of mustard seed ... ," Thielicke had to remind himself.

That image—a handful of saints praying indoors while outside goose-step the legions of power—captures how I often feel. The weapons of faith seem virtually powerless deployed against the forces of ungrace. Can one fight nuclear warheads with a slingshot?

Yet history shows that grace has its own power. Great leaders—Lincoln, Gandhi, King, Rabin, and Sadat come to mind, all of whom paid the ultimate price for defying the law of ungrace—can help create a national climate that leads to reconciliation. How different would modern history be if Sadat and not Saddam had ruled Iraq. Or if a Lincoln emerged from the ruins of the Balkans.

Politics deals with externals: borders, wealth, crimes. Authentic forgiveness deals with the evil in a person's heart, something for which politics has no cure. Virulent evil (racism, ethnic hatred) spreads through society like an airborne disease; one cough infects a whole busload.

The cure, like a vaccine, must be applied one person at a time. When moments of grace do occur, the world must pause, fall silent, and acknowledge that indeed forgiveness offers a kind of cure.

In 1987 an IRA bomb went off in a small town west of Belfast, amid a group of Protestants who had gathered to honor the war dead on Veteran's Day. Eleven people died and sixty-three others were wounded. What made this act of terrorism stand out from so many others was the response of one of the wounded, Gordon Wilson, a devout Methodist who had emigrated north from the Irish Republic to work as a draper. The bomb buried Wilson and his twenty-year-old daughter under five feet of concrete and brick. "Daddy, I love you very much," were the last words Marie spoke, grasping her father's hand as they waited for the rescuers. She suffered severe spinal and brain injuries and died a few hours later in the hospital.

A newspaper later proclaimed, "No one remembers what the politicians had to say at that time. No one who heard Gordon Wilson will ever forget what he confessed.... His grace towered over the miserable justifications of the bombers." Speaking from his hospital bed, Wilson said, "I have lost my daughter, but I bear no grudge. Bitter talk is not going to bring Marie Wilson back to life. I shall pray, tonight and every night, that God will forgive them."

His daughter's last words were words of love, and Gordon Wilson determined to live out his life on that plane of love. "The world wept," said one report, as Wilson gave a similar interview over the BBC radio that week.

After his release from the hospital, Gordon Wilson led a crusade for Protestant-Catholic reconciliation. Protestant extremists who had planned to avenge the bombing decided, because of the publicity surrounding Wilson, that such behavior would be politically foolish. Wilson wrote a book about his daughter, spoke out against violence, and constantly repeated the refrain, "Love is the bottom line." He met with the IRA, personally forgave them for what they had done, and asked them to lay down their arms. "I know that you've lost loved ones, just like me," he told them. "Surely, enough is enough. Enough blood has been spilled."

The Irish Republic ultimately made Wilson a member of its Senate. When he died in 1995, the Irish Republic, Northern Ireland, and all of Great Britain honored this ordinary Christian citizen who had gained fame for his uncommon spirit of grace and forgiveness. His spirit exposed by contrast the violent deeds of retaliation, and his life of peacemaking came to symbolize the craving for peace within many others who would never make the headlines.

"To bless the people who have oppressed our spirits, emotionally deprived us, or in other ways handicapped us, is the most extraordinary work any of us will ever do," writes Elizabeth O'Connor.

During John Paul II's reign as pope another drama of

personal forgiveness captured the world's fleeting attention. John Paul went into the bowels of Rome's Rebibbia prison to visit Mehmet Ali Agca, a hired assassin who had tried to kill him and nearly succeeded. "I forgive you," said the Pope.

Time magazine, impressed by the event, devoted a cover story to it in which Lance Morrow wrote, "John Paul meant, among other things, to demonstrate how the private and public dimensions of human activity may fuse in moral action.... John Paul wanted to proclaim that great issues are determined, or at least informed, by the elemental impulses of the human breast—hatred or love." Morrow went on to quote a Milan newspaper: "There will be no escape from wars, from hunger, from misery, from racial discrimination, from denial of human rights, and not even from missiles, if our hearts are not changed."

Morrow added,

> The scene in Rebibbia had a symbolic splendor. It shone in lovely contrast to what the world has witnessed lately in the news. For some time, a suspicion has taken hold that the trajectory of history is descendent, that the world moves from disorder to greater disorder, toward darkness—or else toward the terminal global flash. The symbolism of the pictures from Rebibbia is precisely the Christian message, that people can be redeemed, that they are ascendant toward the light.

John Paul's deed shone all the more brightly because of its dim setting: a bare concrete cell, the perfect back-drop for the dreary law of unforgiveness. Assassins are to be imprisoned or executed, not forgiven. Yet, for a moment, the message of forgiveness radiated through prison walls, showing the world a path of transformation, not retribution.

The Pope, of course, was following the example of One who did not survive an attempt against his life. Kangaroo courts of Judea found a way to inflict a sentence of capital punishment on the only perfect man who ever lived. From the cross, Jesus pronounced his own counter-sentence, striking an eternal blow against the law of unforgiveness. Notably, he forgave those who had not repented: "for they do not know what they are doing."

The Roman soldiers, Pilate, Herod, and members of the Sanhedrin were "just doing their jobs"—the limp excuse later used to explain Auschwitz, My Lai, and the Gulag—but Jesus stripped away that institutional veneer and spoke to the human heart. It was forgiveness they needed, more than anything else. We know, those of us who believe in the atonement, that Jesus had more than his executioners in mind when he spoke those final words. He had us in mind. In the cross, and only in the cross, he put an end to the law of eternal consequences.

Does forgiveness matter in places around the world where so much evil has been wrought? It must, or the people there will have no hope of living together. As so many abused children learn, without forgiveness we cannot free ourselves from the grip of the past. The same principle applies to nations.

I have a friend whose marriage has gone through tumultuous times. One night George passed a breaking point. He pounded the table and the floor. "I hate you!" he screamed at his wife. "I won't take it anymore! I've had enough! I won't go on! I won't let it happen! No! No! No!"

Several months later my friend woke up in the middle of the night and heard strange sounds coming from the room where his two-year-old son slept. He padded down the hall, stood for a moment outside his son's door, and shivers ran through his flesh. He could not draw a breath. In a soft voice, the two-year-old was repeating word for word with precise inflection the argument between his mother and father. "I hate you.... I won't take it anymore.... No! No! No!"

George realized that in some awful way he had just bequeathed his pain and anger and unforgiveness to the next generation. Is not that what is happening all over the world right now?

Apart from forgiveness, the monstrous past may awake at any time from hibernation to devour the present. And also the future.

Chapter 8

THE ARSENAL
OF GRACE

Walter Wink tells of two peacemakers who visited a group of Polish Christians ten years after the end of World War II. "Would you be willing to meet with other Christians from West Germany?" the peacemakers asked. "They want to ask forgiveness for what Germany did to Poland during the war and to begin to build a new relationship."

At first there was silence. Then one Pole spoke up. "What you are asking is impossible. Each stone of Warsaw is soaked in Polish blood! We cannot forgive!"

Before the group parted, however, they said the Lord's Prayer together. When they reached the words "forgive us our sins as we forgive ...," everyone stopped praying. Tension swelled in the room. The Pole who had spoken so vehemently said, "I must say yes to you. I could no more pray the Our Father, I could no longer call myself a Christian, if I refuse to forgive. Humanly speaking, I cannot do it, but God will give us his strength!" Eighteen months later the Polish and West German Christians met together in Vienna, establishing friendships that continue to this day.

A recent book, *The Wages of Guilt*, explores the differences in approach to war guilt by Germany and Japan. German survivors, like those who apologized to the Poles, tend to accept responsibility for the crimes committed during the war. For example, when Berlin's mayor Willy Brandt visited Warsaw in 1970, he fell to his knees before the memorial to the victims of the Warsaw ghetto. "This gesture ... was not planned," he wrote. "Oppressed by the memories of Germany's recent history, I simply did what people do when words fail them."

In contrast, Japan has been reluctant to acknowledge any guilt over their role in the war. Emperor Hirohito announced Japan's surrender with the classic understatement, "The war situation has developed not necessarily to Japan's advantage," and postwar statements have been just as calculated. The Japanese government declined to attend the fiftieth-anniversary commemoration of Pearl Harbor because the United States made the invitation conditional on an apology. "The entire world is responsible for the war," a cabinet secretary insisted. Not until 1995, in fact, did Japan use the word "apology" about their actions.

Today, German schoolchildren learn details of the

Holocaust and other Nazi crimes. Their counterparts in Japan learn about the atomic bombs dropped on them, but not about the Massacre of Nanking, the brutal treatment of POWs and vivisection of U.S. prisoners, or the foreign "sex slaves" conscripted to serve Japanese soldiers. As a result, resentment still smolders in countries such as China, Korea, and the Philippines.

The contrast must not be pressed too far because both Japan and Germany have gained acceptance in the world of nations, a token of international "forgiveness" for their aggression. Yet Germany has been welcomed as a full partner in the new Europe, side by side with its former victims, whereas Japan is still negotiating arrangements with its cautious former enemies. Its slowness to apologize has delayed the process of full acceptance.

In 1990 the world watched a drama of forgiveness enacted on the stage of world politics. After East Germany chose a parliament in its first free elections, the representatives convened to take up the reins of government. The Communist bloc was changing daily, West Germany was proposing the radical step of reunification, and the new parliament had many weighty matters of state to consider. For their first official act, however, they decided to vote on this extraordinary statement, drafted in the language of theology, not politics:

> We, the first freely elected parliamentarians
> of the GDR ... on behalf of the citizens of this

land, admit responsibility for the humiliation, expulsion and murder of Jewish men, women and children. We feel sorrow and shame, and acknowledge this burden of German history.... Immeasurable suffering was inflicted on the peoples of the world during the era of national socialism.... We ask all the Jews of the world to forgive us. We ask the people of Israel to forgive us for the hypocrisy and hostility of official East German policies toward Israel and for the persecution and humiliation of Jewish citizens in our country after 1945 as well.

East Germany's parliament passed the statement unanimously. Members rose to their feet for a long ovation and then paused for a moment of silence in memory of the Jews who had died in the Holocaust.

What did such an act of parliament accomplish? Certainly it did not bring the murdered Jews back to life or undo the monstrous deeds of Nazism. No, but it helped loosen the stranglehold of guilt that had been choking East Germans for nearly half a century—five decades in which their government had steadfastly denied any need for forgiveness.

For its part, West Germany had already repented officially for the abominations. In addition, West Germany has paid out sixty billion dollars in reparations to Jews. The fact that a relationship exists at all between Germany and Israel is a stunning demonstration of transnational forgiveness. Grace has its own power, even in international politics.

Recent times have seen other public dramas of forgiveness play out in nations formerly controlled by Communists.

In 1983, before the Iron Curtain lifted and during the period of martial law, Pope John Paul II visited Poland, where he conducted a huge open-air mass. Throngs of people, organized in orderly groups by their parishes, marched over the Poniatowski Bridge and streamed toward the stadium. Just before the bridge, the route crossed directly in front of the Communist Party's Central Committee Building, and hour after hour the platoons of marchers chanted in unison, "We forgive you, we forgive you!" as they passed the building. Some said the slogan with heartfelt sincerity. Others shouted it almost with contempt, as if to say, "You're nothing—we don't even hate you."

A few years later Jerzy Popieluszko, a thirty-five-year-old priest whose sermons had electrified Poland, was found floating in the Vistula River with his eyes gouged out and his fingernails torn off. Once again Polish Catholics took to the streets, marching with banners that read "We forgive. We forgive." Popieluszko had preached the same message Sunday after Sunday to the multitude who filled the square in front of his church: "Defend the truth. Overcome evil with good." After his death they continued to obey him, and in the end it was exactly this spirit of prevailing grace that caused the regime to collapse.

All over Eastern Europe the struggle of forgiveness being waged. Should a pastor in Russia forgive the KGB officers who imprisoned him and razed his church? Should Romanians forgive the doctors and nurses who chained sick orphans to their beds? Should citizens of Eastern Germany forgive the stool pigeons—including seminary professors, pastors, and treacherous spouses—who spied on them? When human rights activist Vera Wollenberger learned that it was her husband who had betrayed her to the secret police, resulting in her arrest and exile, she ran to the bathroom and vomited. "I would not want anyone to experience the hell I have been through," she says.

Paul Tillich once defined forgiveness as remembering the past in order that it might be forgotten—a principle that applies to nations as well as individuals. Though forgiveness is never easy, and may take generations, what else can break the chains that enslave people to their historical past?

I will never forget a scene that I witnessed in the Soviet Union in October 1991. I told the story in a small book published just after our visit, but it bears retelling. At the time, the Soviet empire was unraveling, Mikhail Gorbachev was hanging on to his office by a string, and Boris Yeltsin was consolidating power by the day.

I accompanied a delegation of Christians who met with Russia's leaders in response to their plea for help in "restoring morality" to their country.

Although Gorbachev and all the government officials we visited had received us warmly, old-timers in our group warned us to expect different treatment the evening we visited KGB headquarters. A statue of its founder Feliks Dzerzhinsky may have been toppled by crowds from a pedestal outside the building, but his memory lived on inside. A large photo of the notorious man still hung on one wall of our meeting room. Agents, their faces as blank and impassive as their movie stereotypes, stood at attention by the doorway of the wood-paneled auditorium as General Nikolai Stolyarov, Vice-Chairman of the KGB, introduced himself to our delegation. We braced ourselves.

"Meeting with you here tonight," General Stolyarov began, "is a plot twist that could not have been conceived by the wildest fiction writer." He had that right. Then he startled us by saying, "We here in the USSR realize that too often we've been negligent in accepting those of the Christian faith. But political questions cannot be decided until there is sincere repentance, a return to faith by the people. That is the cross I must bear. In the study of scientific atheism, there was the idea that religion divides people. Now we see the opposite: love for God can only unite."

Our heads spun. Where did he learn the phrase "bear

a cross"? And the other word—*repentance?* Did the trans-
lator get that right? I glanced at Peter and Anita Deyneka,
banned from Russia for thirteen years because of their
Christian work, now munching cookies in the KGB
headquarters.

Joel Nederhood, a refined, gentle man who made
radio and television broadcasts for the Christian Reformed
Church, stood with a question for Stolyarov. "General,
many of us have read Solzhenitsyn's report of the Gulag.
A few of us have even lost family members there." His
boldness caught some of his colleagues off guard, and the
tension in the room noticeably thickened. "Your agency,
of course, is responsible for overseeing the prisons, including the one located in the basement of this building. How
do you respond to that past?"

Stolyarov replied in measured tones: "I have spoken of
repentance. This is an essential step. You probably know of
Abuladze's film by that title. There can be no *perestroika*
apart from repentance. The time has come to repent of
that past. We have broken the Ten Commandments, and
for this we pay today."

I had seen *Repentance* by Tengiz Abuladze, and
Stolyarov's allusion to it was stunning. The movie details
false denunciations, forced imprisonment, the burning
of churches—the very acts that had earned the KGB its
reputation for cruelty, especially against religion. In
Stalin's era an estimated 42,000 priests lost their lives,
and the total number of priests declined from 380,000

to 172. A thousand monasteries, sixty seminaries, and ninety-eight of every hundred Orthodox churches were shuttered.

Repentance portrays atrocities from the vantage point of one provincial town. In the film's most poignant scene, women of the village rummage through the mud of a lumberyard inspecting a shipment of logs that has just floated down the river. They are searching for messages from their husbands who have cut these logs in a prison camp. One woman finds initials carved into the bark and, weeping, caresses the log tenderly, her only thread of connection to a husband she cannot caress. The movie ends with a peasant woman asking directions to a church. Told that she is on the wrong street, she replies, "What good is a street that doesn't lead to a church?"

Now, sitting in the state headquarters of tyranny, in a room built just above the detention rooms where Solzhenitsyn was interrogated, we were being told something very similar by the Vice-Chairman of the KGB. What good is a path that doesn't lead to repentance, to the Ten Commandments, to a church?

Abruptly, the meeting took a more personal turn as Alex Leonovich rose to speak. Alex had been sitting at the head table translating for Stolyarov. A native of Byelorussia, he had escaped during Stalin's reign of terror and had emigrated to the United States. For forty-six years he had been broadcasting Christian programs, often jammed, back to the land of his birth. He knew personally many Christians who had been tortured and persecuted for their faith. For him, to be translating such a message of reconciliation from a high official of the KGB was bewildering and nearly incomprehensible.

Alex, a stout, grandfatherly man, epitomizes the old guard of warriors who have prayed for more than half a century that change might come to the Soviet Union—the very change we were apparently now witnessing. He spoke slowly and softly to General Stolyarov.

"General, many members of my family suffered because of this organization," Alex said. "I myself had to leave the land that I loved. My uncle, who was very dear to me, went to a labor camp in Siberia and never returned. General, you say that you repent. Christ taught us how to respond. On behalf of my family, on behalf of my uncle who died in the Gulag, I forgive you."

And then Alex Leonovich, Christian evangelist, reached over to General Nikolai Stolyarov, the Vice-Chairman of the KGB, and gave him a Russian bear hug. While they embraced, Stolyarov whispered something to Alex, and not until later did we learn what he said. "Only two times in my life have I cried. Once was when my mother died. The other is tonight."

"I feel like Moses," Alex said on the bus home that evening. "I have seen the promised land. I am ready for glory."

The Russian photographer accompanying us had a less sanguine view. "It was all an act," he said. "They were putting on a mask for you. I can't believe it." Yet he too wavered, apologizing a short time later: "Maybe I was wrong. I don't know what to believe anymore."

For the next decades—and perhaps centuries—the former Soviet Union will be confronting issues of forgiveness. Afghanistan, Chechnya, Armenia, Ukraine, Latvia, Lithuania, Estonia—each of these states bears a grudge against the empire that dominated them. Each of them will question motives, much like the photographer who accompanied us to KGB headquarters. With good reason, Russians do not trust each other or their government. The past must be remembered before it can be overcome.

Even so, overcoming history is possible, however slowly and imperfectly. The chains of ungrace can indeed snap. We in the United States have had experience with reconciliation on a national scale: archenemies in World War II, Germany and Japan are now two of our staunchest allies. Even more significantly—and of more direct relevance to places like the former Soviet Union and Yugoslavia—we fought a bloody Civil War that set family against family and the nation against itself.

I grew up in Atlanta, Georgia, where attitudes toward General Sherman, who burned Atlanta to the ground, suggest how Bosnian Muslims must feel about their Serbian neighbors. It was Sherman, after all, who introduced the "scorched earth" tactics of modern warfare, a policy that would be perfected in the Balkans. Somehow our nation did survive, as one. Southerners still debate the merits of the Confederate flag and the song "Dixie," but I haven't heard much talk of secession lately or of dividing the nation into ethnic enclaves. Two of our modern Presidents have hailed from Arkansas and Georgia.

After the Civil War, politicians and advisers urged Abraham Lincoln to punish the South severely for all the bloodshed it had caused. "Do I not destroy my enemies when I make them my friends?" replied the President, who instead set forth a magnanimous plan of Reconstruction. Lincoln's spirit guided a nation even after his death, perhaps the central reason the "United" States endured.

Even more impressive are the steps toward reconciliation between white and black races, one of which used to *own* the other. The lingering effects of racism prove that it takes many years and much hard work to undo injustice. Still, every step African Americans take toward participation as citizens implies a move toward forgiveness. Not all blacks forgive and not all whites repent; racism deeply divides this country. Yet compare our situation with what has happened in, say, ex-Yugoslavia or Syria. I haven't seen any machine-gunners blocking the routes to Atlanta or artillery shells raining down on Birmingham.

I grew up a racist. I remember well when the South practiced a perfectly legal form of apartheid. Stores in downtown Atlanta had three rest rooms: White Men,

White Women, and Colored. Gas stations had two drinking fountains, one for Whites and one for Colored. Motels
and restaurants served white patrons only, and when the
Civil Rights Act made such discrimination illegal, many
owners shuttered their establishments.

Lester Maddox, later elected Governor of Georgia,
was one of the protesting restaurateurs. After closing his
fried chicken outlets, he opened a memorial to the death
of freedom, featuring a copy of the Bill of Rights resting
in a black-draped coffin. To support himself he sold clubs
and ax handles in three different sizes—Daddy, Mama,
and Junior—replicas of the clubs used to beat black civil
rights demonstrators. I bought one of those ax handles
with money earned from my paper route. Lester Maddox
sometimes attended my church (his sister was a member),
and it was there I learned a twisted theological basis for
my racism.

In the 1960s the church deacon board mobilized look-
out squads, and on Sundays these took turns patrolling the
entrances lest any black "troublemakers" try to integrate
us. I still have one of the cards the deacons printed up to
give to any civil rights demonstrators who might appear:

> Believing the motives of your group to be ulte-
> rior and foreign to the teaching of God's word,
> *we cannot extend a welcome to you* and respect-
> fully request you to leave the premises quietly.
> Scripture does NOT teach "the brotherhood

of man and the fatherhood of God." He is the Creator of all, but only the Father of those who have been regenerated.

If any one of you is here with a sincere desire to know Jesus Christ as Saviour and Lord, we shall be glad to deal individually with you from the Word of God.

(UNANIMOUS STATEMENT OF PASTOR AND
DEACONS, AUGUST 1960)

When Congress passed the Civil Rights Act, our church founded a private school as a haven for whites, expressly barring all black students. A few "liberal" members left the church in protest when the kindergarten turned down the daughter of a black Bible professor, but most of us approved of the decision. A year later the church board rejected a Carver Bible Institute student for membership (his name was Tony Evans and he went on to become a prominent pastor and speaker).

We used to call Martin Luther King Jr. "Martin Lucifer Coon." We said that King was a card-carrying Communist, a Marxist agent who merely posed as a minister. Not until much later was I able to appreciate the moral strength of the man who, perhaps more than any other person, kept the South from outright racial war.

My white colleagues in school and in church cheered King's televised encounters with southern sheriffs, police dogs, and fire hoses. Little did we know that by doing so we were playing directly into King's strategy. He deliberately sought out individuals like Sheriff Bull Connor and stage-managed scenes of confrontation, accepting beatings, jailings, and other brutalities, because he believed a complacent nation would rally around his cause only when they saw the evil of racism manifest in its ugliest extreme. "Christianity," he used to say, "has always insisted that the cross we bear precedes the crown we wear."

King recorded his struggle with forgiveness in "Letter from Birmingham City Jail." Outside the jail Southern pastors were denouncing him as a Communist, mobs were yelling "Hang the nigger!" and policemen were swinging nightsticks at his unarmed supporters. King writes that he had to fast for several days in order to achieve the spiritual discipline necessary for him to forgive his enemies.

By forcing evil out into the open, King was attempting to tap into a national reservoir of moral outrage, a concept my friends and I were not equipped to understand. Many historians point to one event as the single moment in which the movement attained at last a critical mass of support for the cause of civil rights. It occurred on the bridge outside Selma, Alabama, when Sheriff Jim Clark turned his policemen loose on unarmed black demonstrators.

The mounted troopers spurred their horses at a run into the crowd of marchers, flailing away with their nightsticks, cracking heads and driving bodies to the ground. As whites on the sidelines whooped and cheered, the troopers shot tear gas into the hysterical marchers. Most Americans got their first glimpse of the scene when ABC interrupted its Sunday movie, *Judgment at Nuremberg*, to show footage. What the viewers saw broadcast live from Alabama bore a horrifying resemblance to what they were watching on film from Nazi Germany. Eight days later President Lyndon Johnson submitted the Voting Rights Act of 1965 to the U.S. Congress.

King had developed a sophisticated strategy of war fought with grace, not gunpowder. He never refused to meet with his adversaries. He opposed policies but not personalities. Most importantly, he countered violence with nonviolence, and hatred with love. "Let us not seek to satisfy our thirst for freedom by drinking from the cup of bitterness and hatred," he exhorted his followers. "We must not allow our creative protest to degenerate into physical violence. Again and again, we must rise to the majestic heights of meeting physical force with soul force."

King's associate Andrew Young remembers those turbulent days as a time when they sought to save "black men's bodies and white men's souls." Their real goal, King said, was not to defeat the white man but "to awaken a sense of shame within the oppressor and challenge his false sense of superiority.... The end is reconciliation; the end is redemption; the end is the creation of the beloved community." And that is what Martin Luther King Jr. finally set into motion, even in die-hard racists like me. The power of grace disarmed my own stubborn evil.

Today as I look back on my childhood I feel shame, remorse, and also repentance. It took years for God to break through my armor of blatant racism—I wonder if any of us sheds its more subtle forms—and I now see that sin as one of the most malevolent, with perhaps the greatest societal impact. I hear much talk these days about the underclass and the crisis in urban America. Experts blame in turn drugs, a decline in values, poverty, and the breakdown of the nuclear family. I wonder if all those problems are consequences of a deeper, underlying cause: our centuries-old sin of racism.

Despite the moral and social fallout from racism, somehow the nation did stay together, and people of all colors eventually joined the democratic process, even in the South. For some years now, Atlanta has elected African-American mayors. And in 1976 Americans saw the extraordinary scene of George Wallace appearing before the black leadership of Alabama to apologize for his past behavior to blacks, an apology he repeated on statewide television.

Wallace's appearance—he needed black votes in a tight race for Governor—was easier to understand than the response to it. Black leaders accepted his apology, and black citizens forgave him, voting for him in droves. When Wallace went on to apologize to the Baptist Church in Montgomery where King had launched the civil rights movement, the leaders who came to offer him forgiveness included Coretta Scott King, Jesse Jackson, and the brother of the murdered Medgar Evers.

Even my childhood church learned to repent. As the neighborhood changed, attendance at that church began to decline. When I attended a service several years ago, I was shocked to find only a few hundred worshipers scattered in the large sanctuary that, in my childhood, used to be packed with fifteen hundred. The church seemed cursed, blighted. It had tried new pastors and new programs, but nothing worked. Though the leaders sought African-American participation, few in the neighborhood responded.

Finally the pastor, a classmate of mine from childhood, took the unusual step of scheduling a service of repentance. In advance of the service he wrote to Tony Evans and to the Bible professor, asking their forgiveness. Then publicly, painfully, with African-American leaders present, he recounted the sin of racism as it had been practiced by the church in the past. He confessed—and received their forgiveness.

Although a burden seemed to lift from the congregation after that service, it was not sufficient to save the church. A few years later the white congregation moved out to the suburbs, and today a rousing African-American congregation, The Wings of Faith, fills the building and rattles its windows once more.

Elton Trueblood notes that the image Jesus used to describe the church's destiny—"The gates of hell will not prevail against it"—is a metaphor of offense, not defense. Christians are storming the gates, and they will prevail. No matter how it looks at any given point in history, the gates guarding the powers of evil will not withstand an assault by grace.

Newspapers prefer to fixate on violent warfare: bombings in Israel and London, assassination squads in Latin America, terrorism in India, Sri Lanka, and Algeria. These produce the grisly images of bleeding faces and amputated limbs that we have come to expect in this most violent of all centuries. And yet no one can deny the power of grace.

Who can forget the images from the Philippines, when common people knelt before fifty-ton tanks, which lurched to a halt as if colliding with an invisible shield of prayer? The Philippines is the only Christian-majority country in Asia, and it was here that the weapons of grace overcame the weapons of tyranny. When Benigno Aquino stepped off the plane in Manila, just before his assassination, he had a speech in his hand with this quote from Gandhi: "The willing sacrifice of the innocent is the most powerful answer to insolent tyranny that has yet been conceived by God or man." Aquino never got the chance to deliver that speech, but his life—and his wife's—proved those words prophetic. The Marcos regime suffered a fatal blow.

The Cold War, says former Senator Sam Nunn, ended "not in a nuclear inferno, but in a blaze of candles in the churches of Eastern Europe." Candlelight processions in East Germany did not show up well on the evening news, but they helped change the face of the globe. First a few hundred, then a thousand, then thirty thousand, fifty thousand, and finally five hundred thousand—nearly the entire population of the city—turned out in Leipzig for candlelight vigils. After a prayer meeting at St. Nikolai Church, the peaceful protestors would march through the dark streets, singing hymns. Police and soldiers with all their weapons seemed powerless against such a force. Ultimately, on the night a similar march in East Berlin attracted one million protestors, the hated Berlin Wall came tumbling down without a shot being fired. A huge banner appeared across a Leipzig street: *Wir danken Dir, Kirche* (We thank you, church).

Like a gale of pure air driving out stagnant clouds of pollution, peaceful revolution spread across the globe. In 1989 alone ten nations—Poland, East Germany, Hungary, Czechoslovakia, Bulgaria, Romania, Albania, Yugoslavia, Mongolia, the Soviet Union—comprising half a billion people experienced nonviolent revolutions. In many of these, the Christian minority played a crucial role. Stalin's mocking question, "How many divisions has the Pope?" got its answer.

Then in 1994 came the most surprising revolution of all, surprising because nearly everyone expected bloodshed. South Africa, though, was also the mother lode of peaceful protest, for it was there that Mohandas Gandhi, studying Tolstoy and the Sermon on the Mount, developed his strategy of nonviolence (which Martin Luther

King Jr. later adopted). With much opportunity to practice, South Africans had perfected the use of the weapons of grace. Walter Wink tells of a black woman who was walking on the street with her children when a white man spat in her face. She stopped, and said, "Thank you, and now for the children." Nonplussed, the man was unable to respond.

In one squatter's village, black South African women suddenly found themselves surrounded by soldiers with bulldozers. The soldiers announced through a bullhorn that the residents had two minutes to clear out before their village would be razed. The women had no weapons, and the men of the village were away at work. Knowing the puritanical tendencies of rural Dutch Reformed Afrikaners, the black women stood in front of the bulldozers and stripped off all their clothes. The police fled, and the village remains standing to this day.

News reports barely mentioned the key role that Christian faith played in South Africa's peaceful revolution. After a mediation team led by Henry Kissinger had abandoned all hope of convincing the Inkatha Freedom Party to participate in elections, a Christian diplomat from Kenya met privately with all the principals, prayed with them, and helped change their minds. (A mysteriously malfunctioning compass on an airplane delayed one flight, making this crucial meeting possible.)

Nelson Mandela broke the chain of ungrace when he emerged from twenty-six years of imprisonment with a message of forgiveness and reconciliation, not revenge. F. W. De Klerk himself, elected from the smallest and most strictly Calvinistic of the South African churches, felt what he later described as "a strong sense of calling." He told his congregation that God was calling him to save all the people of South Africa, even though he knew that would mean rejection by his own people.

Black leaders insisted that De Klerk apologize for racial apartheid. He balked, because the people who had started the policy included his own father. But Bishop Desmond Tutu believed it essential that the process of reconciliation in South Africa begin with forgiveness, and he would not relent. According to Tutu, "One lesson we should be able to teach the world, and that we should be able to teach the people of Bosnia, Rwanda, and Burundi, is that we are ready to forgive." Eventually, De Klerk did apologize.

Now that the black majority has political power, they are formally considering issues of forgiveness. The minister of justice sounds downright theological as he formulates a policy. No one can forgive on behalf of victims, he says; victims have to forgive for themselves. And no one can forgive without full disclosure: what happened and who did what must first be revealed. Also, those who committed the atrocities must agree to ask for forgiveness before it can be granted. Step by step, South Africans are remembering their past in order to forget it.

Forgiveness is neither easy nor clear-cut, as South

Africans are finding out. The pope may forgive his assassin but not ask for his release from prison. One may forgive the Germans but put restrictions on the armies, forgive a child abuser but keep him away from his victims, forgive Southern racism but enforce laws to keep it from happening again.

Yet nations that pursue forgiveness, in all its complexity, may at least avoid the awful consequences of the alternative—unforgiveness. Instead of scenes of massacre and civil war, the world was treated to the sight of black South Africans in long, snaking lines that stretched in some cases for more than a mile, *dancing* in jubilation over their first-ever opportunity to vote.

Because it goes against human nature, forgiveness must be taught and practiced, as one would practice any difficult craft. "Forgiveness is not just an occasional act: it is a permanent attitude," said Martin Luther King Jr. What greater gift could Christians give to the world than the forming of a culture that upholds grace and forgiveness?

The Benedictines, for example, have a moving service of forgiveness and reconciliation. After giving instruction from the Bible, the leaders ask each one attending to identify issues that require forgiveness. Worshipers then submerge their hands in a large crystal bowl of water, "holding" the grievance in their cupped hands. As they pray for the grace to forgive, gradually their hands open to symbolically "release" the grievance. "Enacting a ceremony like this with one's body," says Bruce Demarest, a participant, "possesses more transforming power than merely uttering the words, 'I forgive.'" What impact might it have if blacks and whites in South Africa—or in the United States of America—plunged their hands repeatedly into a common bowl of forgiveness?

In his book *The Prisoner and the Bomb*, Laurens van der Post recounts the misery of his wartime experiences in a Japanese prison camp in Java. In that unlikely place he concluded,

> The only hope for the future lay in an all-embracing attitude of forgiveness of the peoples who had been our enemies. Forgiveness, my prison experience had taught me, was not mere religious sentimentality; it was as fundamental a law of the human spirit as the law of gravity. If one broke the law of gravity one broke one's neck; if one broke this law of forgiveness one inflicted a mortal wound on one's spirit and became once again a member of the chain-gang of mere cause and effect from which life has laboured so long and painfully to escape.

Chapter 9

THE GRACE-FULL CHRISTIAN

Simone Weil's life flamed like a bright candle before she died at the age of thirty-three. A French intellectual, she chose to work on farms and in factories in order to identify with the working class. When Hitler's armies rolled into France, she escaped to join the Free French in London, and there she died, her tuberculosis complicated by malnourishment when she refused to eat more than the rations of her countrymen suffering Nazi occupation. As her only legacy, this Jew who followed Christ left in scattered notes and journals a dense record of her pilgrimage toward God.

Weil concluded that two great forces rule the universe: gravity and grace. Gravity causes one body to attract other bodies so that it continually enlarges by absorbing more and more of the universe into itself. Something like this same force operates in human beings. We too want to expand, to acquire, to swell in significance. The desire to "be as gods," after all, led Adam and Eve to rebel.

Emotionally, Weil concluded, we humans operate by laws as fixed as Newton's. "All the *natural* movements of the soul are controlled by laws analogous to those of physical gravity. Grace is the only exception." Most of us remain trapped in the gravitational field of self-love, and thus we "fill up all the fissures through which grace might pass."

About the same time Weil was writing, another refugee from the Nazis, Karl Barth, made the comment that Jesus' gift of forgiveness, of grace, was to him more astonishing than Jesus' miracles. Miracles broke the physical laws of the universe; forgiveness broke the moral rules. "The beginning of good is perceived in the midst of bad.... The simplicity and comprehensiveness of grace—who shall measure it?"

Who shall measure it indeed? I have merely walked the perimeter of grace, as one walks around a cathedral far too large and grand to behold at one glance. I now end with a final question: What does a grace-full Christian look like?

Perhaps I should rephrase the question, How does a grace-full Christian *look*? The Christian life, I believe, does not primarily center on ethics or rules but rather involves a new way of seeing. I escape the force of spiritual "gravity" when I begin to see myself as a sinner who cannot please God by any method of self-improvement or self-enlargement. Only then can I turn to God for outside help—for grace—and to my amazement I learn that a holy God already loves me despite my defects. I escape the force of gravity again when I recognize my neighbors also as sinners, loved by God. A grace-full Christian is one who looks at the world through "grace-tinted lenses."

A pastor friend of mine was studying the assigned text for the day from Matthew 7 in which Jesus said, rather fiercely, "Many will say to me on that day, 'Lord, Lord, did we not prophesy in your name, and in your name drive out demons and perform many miracles?' Then I will tell them plainly, 'I never knew you. Away from me, you evildoers!'"

The phrase "I never knew you" leaped out from the page. Pointedly, Jesus did not say "*You* never knew *me*," or "You never knew the Father." It struck my friend that one of our main tasks, perhaps the main task, is to make ourselves known to God. Good works are not enough— "Did we not prophesy in your name?"—any relationship with God must be based on full disclosure. The masks must come off.

"We cannot find Him unless we know we need Him," wrote Thomas Merton. For someone raised in a strong church background, that awareness may not come easily. My own church tended toward perfectionism, which tempted us all to follow the example of Ananias and Sapphira in misrepresenting ourselves spiritually. On Sundays well-scrubbed families emerged from their cars with smiles on their faces even though, as we later found out, they had been fighting abusively all week long.

As a child, I put on my best behavior on Sunday mornings, dressing up for God and for the Christians around me. It never occurred to me that church was a place to be honest. Now, though, as I seek to look at the world through the lens of grace, I realize that imperfection is the prerequisite for grace. Light only gets in through the cracks.

My pride still tempts me to put on the best front, to clean up appearances. "It is easy to acknowledge," said C. S. Lewis, "but almost impossible to realise for long, that we are mirrors whose brightness, if we are bright, is wholly derived from the sun that shines upon us. Surely we must have a little—however little—native luminosity? Surely we can't be *quite* creatures." He goes on, "Grace substitutes a full, childlike and delighted acceptance of our Need, a joy in total dependence. We become 'jolly beggars.'"

We creatures, we jolly beggars, give glory to God by our dependence. Our wounds and defects are the very fissures through which grace might pass. It is our human destiny on earth to be imperfect, incomplete, weak, and mortal, and only by accepting that destiny can we escape the force of gravity and receive grace. Only then can we grow close to God.

Strangely, God is closer to sinners than to "saints." (By saints I mean those people renowned for their piety—true saints never lose sight of their sinfulness.) As one lecturer in spirituality explains it, "God in heaven holds each person by a string. When you sin, you cut the string. Then God ties it up again, making a knot—and thereby bringing you a little closer to him. Again and again your sins cut the string—and with each further knot God keeps drawing you closer and closer."

Once my view of myself changed, I began to see the church in a different light too: as a community of people thirsty for grace. Like alcoholics on the path to recovery, we share a mutually acknowledged weakness. Gravity tempts us to believe we can make it on our own; grace corrects that error.

God needs humble people (which usually means *humbled* people) to accomplish his work. Whatever makes us feel superior to other people, whatever tempts us to convey a sense of superiority, that is gravity, not grace.

Readers of the Gospels marvel at Jesus' ability to move with ease among the sinners and outcasts. Having spent time around "sinners" and also around purported "saints," I have a hunch why Jesus spent so much time with the former group: I think he preferred their company.

Because the sinners were honest about themselves and had no pretense, Jesus could deal with them. In contrast, the saints put on airs, judged him, and sought to catch him in a moral trap. In the end it was the saints, not the sinners, who arrested Jesus.

Recall the story of Jesus' dinner at the home of Simon the Pharisee, in which a woman not so different from a common prostitute poured perfume on Jesus and provocatively wiped his feet with her hair. Simon was repulsed—such a woman did not even deserve to enter his house! Here is how Jesus responded in that tense atmosphere:

> Then he turned toward the woman and said to Simon, "Do you see this woman? I came into your house. You did not give me any water for my feet, but she wet my feet with her tears and wiped them with her hair. You did not give me a kiss, but this woman, from the time I entered, has not stopped kissing my feet. You did not put oil on my head, but she has poured perfume on my feet. Therefore, I tell you, her many sins have been forgiven—for she loved much. But he who has been forgiven little loves little."

Why is it, I ask myself, that the church sometimes conveys the spirit of Simon the Pharisee rather than that of the forgiven woman? Why is it that I too often fail the grace test?

A novel published more than a century ago, *The Damnation of Theron Ware*, gave me a lasting image of what the church should be. A skeptical doctor speaking to a fundamentalist pastor and a Catholic priest said, "If you don't mind my saying so—of course I view you all impartially from the outside—but it seems logical to me that a church should exist for those who need its help, and not for those who by their own profession are so good already that it is they who help the church." The skeptic then described church as a place that should keep grace on tap. "Some come every day, some only once a year, some perhaps never between their baptism and their funeral. But they all have a right here, the professional burglar every whit as much as the speckless saint. The only stipulation is that they oughtn't to come under false pretenses. ..."

That image of church dispensing grace "on tap" has special poignancy for me because of an AA group that met in the basement of my church in Chicago. Alcoholics Anonymous can't get many churches to loan their facilities, for a very practical reason: their groups tend to make a mess. AA members fight off the demons of addiction to drugs and alcohol by relying on lesser demons of cigarettes and coffee, and few churches want to put up with the stains on floors and tables and the smoke damage to walls and drapes. The church I attended decided to open their doors to AA regardless.

I sometimes attended AA as an act of solidarity with a recovering alcoholic friend. The first time I accompanied him I was overwhelmed by what I found, for in many ways it resembled the New Testament church. A well-known television broadcaster and several prominent millionaires mixed freely with unemployed dropouts and kids who wore Band-Aids to hide the needle marks on their arms. The "sharing time" was like a textbook small group, marked by compassionate listening, warm responses, and many hugs. Introductions went like this: "Hi, I'm Tom, and I'm an alcoholic and a drug addict." Instantly everyone shouted out in unison, like a Greek chorus, "Hi, Tom!" Each person attending gave a personal progress report on his or her battle with addiction.

Over time I saw that AA runs on two principles: radical honesty and radical dependence. These are the very same principles expressed in the Lord's Prayer, Jesus' capsule summary of living "one day at a time," and in fact many AA groups recite the Lord's Prayer together at each meeting.

AA would never allow a person to say, "Hi, I'm Tom, I used to be an alcoholic but now I'm cured." Even if Tom has not had a drink for thirty years, he still must identify himself as an alcoholic—by denying his weakness he would make himself its victim. Also, Tom could never say, "I may be an alcoholic, but I'm not as bad as Betty there. She's a cocaine addict." In AA the ground is level.

As Lewis Meyer puts it,

It is the only place I know where status means nothing. Nobody fools anybody else. Everyone is here because he or she made a slobbering mess of his or her life and is trying to put the pieces back together again. . . . I have attended thousands of church meetings, lodge meetings, brotherhood meetings—yet I have never found the kind of love I find at AA. For one small hour the high and mighty descend and the lowly rise. The leveling that results is what people mean when they use the word brotherhood.

For a "cure," the AA program demands of its members radical dependence on a Higher Power and on fellow stragglers. Most people in the groups I've attended substitute "God" for "Higher Power." They openly ask God for forgiveness and strength, and ask their friends around them for support. They come to AA because they believe that there, grace flows "on tap."

Sometimes as I went up and down the stairs connecting our church sanctuary to the basement, I thought of the upstairs/downstairs contrast between Sunday mornings and Tuesday evenings. Only a few of those who met on Tuesday evenings returned on Sundays. Though they appreciated the church's generosity in opening its basement to them, the AA members I talked with said they would not feel at ease in church. Upstairs people seemed to have it together, while they were just barely hanging on. They felt more comfortable in the swirl of blue smoke, slouched in metal chairs in jeans and a T-shirt, using swear words if they felt like it. That's where they belonged, not in a stained-glass sanctuary with straight-backed pews.

If only they realized, if only the church could realize, that in some of the most important lessons of spirituality, members of the basement group were our masters. They began with radical honesty and ended with radical dependence. Athirst, they came as "jolly beggars" every week because AA was the one place that offered grace on tap.

A few times at my church I preached the sermon, then assisted in the ceremony of Communion. "I don't partake because I'm a good Catholic, holy and pious and sleek," writes Nancy Mairs about the Eucharist. "I partake because I'm a bad Catholic, riddled by doubt and anxiety and anger: fainting from severe hypoglycemia of the soul." After delivering the sermon, I helped nourish famished souls.

At my church, those who desired to partake would come to the front, stand quietly in a semicircle, and wait for us to bring them the elements. "The body of Christ broken for you," I would say as I held out a loaf of bread for the person before me to break off. "The blood of Christ shed for you," the pastor behind me would say, holding out a common cup.

Because my wife worked for the church, and because I taught a class there for many years, I knew the stories of some of the people standing before me. I knew that Mabel, the woman with strawy hair and bent posture who came to the senior citizen's center, had been a prostitute. My wife worked with her for seven years before Mabel confessed the dark secret buried deep within. Fifty years ago she had sold her only child, a daughter. Her family had rejected her long before, the pregnancy had eliminated her source of income, and she knew she would make a terrible mother, and so she sold the baby to a couple in Michigan. She could never forgive herself, she said. Now she was standing at the Communion rail, spots of rouge like paper discs pasted on her cheeks, her hands outstretched, waiting to receive the gift of grace. "The body of Christ broken for you, Mabel . . ."

Beside Mabel were Gus and Mildred, star players in the only wedding ceremony ever performed among the church's seniors. They lost $150 per month in Social Security benefits by marrying rather than living together, but Gus insisted. He said Mildred was the light of his life, and he didn't care if he lived in poverty as long as he lived it with her at his side. "The blood of Christ shed for you, Gus, and you, Mildred . . ."

Next came Adolphus, an angry young black man whose worst fears about the human race had been confirmed in Vietnam. Adolphus scared people away from our church. Once, in a class I was teaching on the book of Joshua, Adolphus raised his hand and pronounced, "I wish I had an M16 rifle right now. I would kill all you white honkeys in this room." An elder in the church who was a doctor took him aside afterwards and talked to him, insisting that he take his medication before services on Sunday. The church put up with Adolphus because we knew he came not merely out of anger but out of hunger. If he missed the bus, and no one had offered him a ride, sometimes he walked five miles to get to church. "The body of Christ broken for you, Adolphus . . ."

I smiled at Christina and Reiner, an elegant German couple employed by the University of Chicago. Both were Ph.D.s, and they came from the same Pietist community in southern Germany. They had told us about the worldwide impact of the Moravian movement, which still influenced their church back home, but right now they were struggling with the very message they held dear. Their son had just left on a mission trip to India. He planned to live for a year in the worst slum in Calcutta. Christina and Reiner had always honored such personal sacrifice—but now that it was their son, everything looked different. They feared for his health and safety. Christina held her face in her hands, and tears dribbled through her fingers. "The blood of Christ shed for you, Christina, and you, Reiner . . ."

Then came Sarah, a turban covering her bare head, scarred from where doctors had removed a brain tumor. And Michael, who stuttered so badly he would physically cringe whenever anyone addressed him. And Maria, the wild and overweight Italian woman who had just married for the fourth time. "Thees one will be deeferent, I just know."

"The body of Christ . . . the blood of Christ . . ." What could we offer such people other than grace, on tap? What better can the church ever offer than "means of grace"? Grace here, among these shattered families and half-coping individuals? Yes, here. Maybe the upstairs church was not so different from the downstairs AA group after all.

Strangely enough, the lens of grace reveals those outside the church in the very same light. Like me, like everyone inside the church, they too are sinners loved by God. Lost children, some have strayed very far from home, but even so the Father stands ready to welcome them back with joy and celebration.

Diviners in a desert, modern artists and thinkers search in vain for alternate sources of grace. "What the world needs, I am ashamed to say, is Christian love," wrote Bertrand Russell. Not long before she died, the secular humanist and novelist Marghanita Laski told a television interviewer, "What I envy most about you Christians is your forgiveness. I have nobody to forgive me." And Douglas Coupland, who coined the term *Generation X*, concluded in his book *Life After God*, "My secret is that I need God—that I am sick and can no longer make it alone. I need God to help me give, because I no longer seem to be capable of giving; to help me be kind, as I no longer seem capable of kindness; to help me love, as I seem beyond being able to love."

I marvel at Jesus' tenderness in dealing with people who expressed such longings. John gives the account of Jesus' impromptu conversation with a woman at a well. In those days the husband initiated divorce: this Samaritan woman had been dumped by five different men. Jesus could have begun by pointing out what a mess the woman had made of her life. Yet he did not say, "Young woman, do you realize what an immoral thing you're doing, living with a man who is not your husband?" Rather he said, in effect, *I sense you are very thirsty*. Jesus went on to tell her that the water she was drinking would never satisfy and then offered her living water to quench her thirst forever.

I try to recall this spirit of Jesus when I encounter someone of whom I morally disapprove. *This must be a very thirsty person*, I tell myself. I once talked with the priest Henri Nouwen just after he had returned from San Francisco. He had visited various ministries to AIDS victims and was moved with compassion by their sad stories. "They want love so bad, it's literally killing them," he said. He saw them as thirsty people panting after the wrong kind of water.

When I am tempted to recoil in horror from sinners, from "different" people, I remember what it must have been like for Jesus to live on earth. Perfect, sinless, Jesus had every right to be repulsed by the behavior of those around them. Yet he treated notorious sinners with mercy and not judgment.

One who has been touched by grace will no longer look on those who stray as "those evil people" or "those poor people who need our help." Nor must we search for signs of "loveworthiness." Grace teaches us that God loves because of who God is, not because of who we are. Categories of worthiness do not apply. In his autobiography, the German philosopher Friedrich Nietzsche told of his ability to "smell" the inmost parts of every soul, especially the "abundant hidden dirt at the bottom of many a character." Nietzsche was a master of ungrace. We are called to do the opposite, to smell the residue of hidden worth.

In a scene from the movie *Ironweed*, the characters played by Jack Nicholson and Meryl Streep stumble across an old Eskimo woman lying in the snow, probably drunk. Besotted themselves, the two debate what they should do about her.

"Is she drunk or a bum?" asks Nicholson.

"Just a bum. Been one all her life."

"And before that?"

"She was a whore in Alaska."

"She hasn't been a whore all her life. Before that?"

"I dunno. Just a little kid, I guess."

"Well, a little kid's something. It's not a bum and it's not a whore. It's something. Let's take her in."

The two vagrants were seeing the Eskimo woman through the lens of grace. Where society saw only a bum and a whore, grace saw "a little kid," a person made in the image of God no matter how defaced that image had become.

Christianity has a principle, "Hate the sin but love the sinner," which is more easily preached than practiced. If Christians could simply recover that practice, modeled so exquisitely by Jesus, we would go a long way toward fulfilling our calling as dispensers of God's grace. For a long time, C. S. Lewis reports, he could never understand the hairsplitting distinction between hating a person's sin and hating the sinner. How could you hate what a man did and not hate the man?

> But years later it occurred to me that there was one man to whom I had been doing this all my life—namely myself. However much I might dislike my own cowardice or conceit or greed, I went on loving myself. There had never been the slightest difficulty about it. In fact the very reason why I hated the things was that I loved the man. Just because I loved myself, I was sorry to find that I was the sort of man who did those things.

Christians should not compromise in hating sin, says Lewis. Rather we should hate the sins in others in the same way we hate them in ourselves: being sorry the person has done such things and hoping that somehow, sometime, somewhere, that person will be cured.

Bill Moyers' documentary film on the hymn "Amazing Grace" includes a scene filmed in Wembley Stadium in London. Various musical groups, mostly rock bands, had gathered together in celebration of the changes in South Africa, and for some reason the promoters scheduled an opera singer, Jessye Norman, as the closing act.

The film cuts back and forth between scenes of the unruly crowd in the stadium and Jessye Norman being interviewed. For twelve hours rock groups like have blasted the crowd through banks of speakers, riling up fans already high on booze and dope. The crowd yells for more curtain calls, and the bands oblige. Meanwhile, Jessye Norman sits in her dressing room discussing "Amazing Grace" with Moyers.

The hymn was written, of course, by John Newton, a coarse, cruel slave trader. He first called out to God in the midst of a storm that nearly threw him overboard. Newton came to see the light only gradually, continuing to ply his trade even after his conversion. He wrote the song "How Sweet the Name of Jesus Sounds" while waiting in an African harbor for a shipment of slaves. Later, though, he renounced his profession, became a minister, and joined William Wilberforce in the fight against slavery. John Newton never lost sight of the depths from which he had been lifted. He never lost sight of grace. When he wrote "… That saved a wretch like me," he meant those words with all his heart.

In the film, Jessye Norman tells Bill Moyers that

Newton may have borrowed an old tune sung by the slaves themselves, redeeming the song, just as he had been redeemed.

Finally, the time comes for her to sing. A single circle of light follows Norman, a majestic African-American woman wearing a flowing African dashiki, as she strolls onstage. No backup band, no musical instruments, just Jessye. The crowd stirs, restless. Few recognize the opera diva. A voice yells for Dire Straits. Others take up the cry. The scene is getting ugly.

Alone, *a capella*, Jessye Norman begins to sing, very slowly:

> Amazing grace, how sweet the sound
> That saved a wretch like me!
> I once was lost but now am found—
> Was blind, but now I see.

A remarkable thing happens in Wembley Stadium that night. Seventy thousand raucous fans fall silent before her aria of grace.

By the time Norman reaches the second verse, "'Twas grace that taught my heart to fear, And grace my fears relieved . . . ," the soprano has the crowd in her hands.

By the time she reaches the third verse, "'Tis grace has brought me safe this far, And grace will lead me home," several thousand fans are singing along, digging far back in nearly lost memories for words they heard long ago.

When we've been there ten thousand years,
    Bright shining as the sun,
We've no less days to sing God's praise
    Than when we first begun.

Jessye Norman later confessed she had no idea what power descended on Wembley Stadium that night. I think I know. The world thirsts for grace. When grace descends, the world falls silent before it.

SOURCES

CHAPTER 1

3 "*Lewis*": C. S. Lewis, *Mere Christianity* in *The Complete C. S. Lewis Signature Classics*. New York: HarperOne, 2002, p. 98.

4 "*Tutu*": Quoted in Marina Cantacuzino, *The Forgiveness Project: Stories for a Vengeful Age*. London: Jessica Kingsley Publishers, 2015, p. viii.

5 "*Not forgiving*": Anne Lamott, *Traveling Mercies: Some Thoughts on Faith*. New York: Pantheon Books, 1999, p. 134.

5 "*Forgiveness means*": Anne Lamott, *Plan B: Further Thoughts on Faith*. New York: Riverhead Books, 2005, p. 47.

6 "*Father, forgive them*": Luke 23:34.

6 "*You have heard*": Matthew 5:43–48.

7 "*Wright*": N. T. Wright, *Evil and the Justice of God*. Downers Grove, Ill.: InterVarsity Press, 2006, p. 136.

8 "*Feed my sheep*": John 21:17.

CHAPTER 2

14 *"This my son"*: Luke 15:24, Revised Standard Version.

14 *"But while"*: Luke 15:20.

15 *"In the same way"*: Luke 15:10.

15 *"Nouwen"*: Henri J. M. Nouwen, *The Return of the Prodigal Son*. New York: Doubleday/Image, 1994, p. 114.

17 *"God, have mercy"*: Luke 18:13.

17 *"There will be more"*: Luke 15:7.

17 *"Jesus, remember"*: Luke 23:42 – 43.

18 *"Kierkegaard"*: Søren Kierkegaard, *Training in Christianity*. Princeton: Princeton University Press, 1947, p. 20.

20 *"This my son was dead"*: Luke 15:32.

CHAPTER 3

21 *"How many times"*: Matthew 18:21–22.

22 *"Pay back"*: Matthew 18:28.

23 *"Lewis"*: C. S. Lewis, "On Forgiveness," in *The Weight of Glory and Other Addresses*. New York: Collier Books/Macmillan, 1980, p. 125.

23 *"Lewis himself"*: C. S. Lewis and Don Giovanni Calabria, *Letters*. Ann Arbor, Mich.: Servant Books, 1988, p. 67.

23 *"Volf"*: Miroslav Volf, *Exclusion and Embrace*. Nashville: Abingdon Press, 1996, p. 85.

24 *"For my thoughts"*: Isaiah 55:8 – 9.

25 *"You do not stay"*: Micah 7:18.

25 *"Swords will flash"*: Hosea 11:6 – 9.

25 *"Go, show your love"*: Hosea 3:1.

26 *"But where sin increased"*: Romans 5:20.

27 *"Buechner"*: Frederick Buechner, *The Longing for Home*. San Francisco: HarperCollins, 1996, p. 175.

27 *"Sayers"*: Dorothy L. Sayers, *Christian Letters to a Post-Christian World*. Grand Rapids: Eerdmans, 1969, p. 45.

28 *"Dr. Bob Smith"*: Story recounted in Ernest Kurtz, *The Spirituality of Imperfection*. New York: Bantam, 1994, pp. 105 – 6.

31 *"Donne"*: John Donne, *John Donne's Sermons on the Psalms and the Gospels*. Berkeley: University of California Press, 1963, p. 22.

33 *"God of all grace"*: 1 Peter 5:10.

CHAPTER 4

41 *"lost coin, lost sheep"*: Luke 15:20.

42 *"Missionary in Lebanon"*: Kenneth E. Bailey, *Poet & Peasant*. Grand Rapids: Eerdmans, 1976, pp. 161 – 64, 181.

CHAPTER 5

46 *"Tolstoy"*: William L. Shirer, *Love and Hatred: The Stormy Marriage of Leo and Sonya Tolstoy*. New York: Simon & Schuster, 1994, pp. 26, 65 – 67.

47 *"Auden"*: W. H. Auden, "September 1, 1939," in *Selected Poems*. New York: Vintage Books/ Random House, 1979, p. 86.

48 *"O'Connor"*: Elizabeth O'Connor, *Cry Pain, Cry Hope*. Waco, Tex.: Word Books, 1987, p. 167.

48 *"Bombeck"*: Erma Bombeck, *At Wit's End*. N. p.: Thorndike Large Print Edition, 1984, p. 63.

49 *"Forgive us"*: Matthew 6:12, King James Version.

49 *"Williams"*: Charles Williams, *The Forgiveness of Sins*. Grand Rapids: Eerdmans, 1984, p. 66.

49 *"If you do not"*: Matthew 6:15.

49 *"Dryden"*: Louis I. Bredvold, ed., *The Best of Dryden*. New York: T. Nelson and Sons, 1933, p. 20.

50 *"Therefore, if you are offering"*: Matthew 5:23–24.

50 *"This is how"*: Matthew 18:35.

51 *"that you may be sons"*: Matthew 5:44–47.

52 *"Bonhoeffer"*: Dietrich Bonhoeffer, *The Cost of Discipleship*. New York: Macmillan, 1959, pp. 134–35.

55 *"Thielicke"*: Helmut Thielicke, *The Waiting Father*. San Francisco: Harper & Row, 1959, p. 133.

56 *"Nouwen"*: Henri Nouwen, *Return*, op. cit., pp. 129–30.

57 *"Do not take revenge"*: Romans 12:19.

CHAPTER 6

63 *"Luther"*: Quoted in "Colorful Sayings of Colorful Luther," in *Christian History*, vol. 34, p. 27.

63 *"Márquez"*: Gabriel García Márquez, *Love in the*

Time of Cholera. New York: Alfred A. Knopf, 1988, pp. 28–30.

63 *"Mauriac"*: François Mauriac, *Knot of Vipers*. London: Metheun, 1984.

64 *"Karr"*: Mary Karr, *The Liars' Club*. New York: Viking, 1995.

66 *"Smedes"*: Lewis B. Smedes, *Shame and Grace*. San Francisco: HarperCollins, 1993, pp. 80, 31.

67 *"Trapp"*: Kathryn Watterson, *Not by the Sword*. New York: Simon & Schuster, 1995.

68 *"Hugo"*: Victor Hugo, *Les Misérables*. New York: Penguin, 1976, p. 111.

70 *"Smedes"*: Lewis B. Smedes, "Forgiveness: the Power to Change the Past," in *Christianity Today*, January 7, 1983, p. 24.

73 *"Weil"*: Simone Weil, *Gravity and Grace*. New York: Routledge, 1972, p. 9.

77 *"We do not have"*: Hebrews 4:15.

77 *"God made him"*: 2 Corinthians 5:21.

77 *"If it is possible"*: Matthew 26:39.

77 *"Forgive them"*: Luke 23:34.

CHAPTER 7

79 *"Wiesenthal"*: Simon Wiesenthal, *The Sunflower*. New York: Schocken, 1976.

85 *"Klausner"*: Joseph Klausner, *Jesus of Nazareth: His Life, Times, and Teaching*. London: George Allen & Unwin, 1925, p. 393.

88 "*Smedes*": Lewis B. Smedes, *Forgive and Forget*. San Francisco: Harper & Row, 1984, p. 130.

89 "*Guardini*": Romano Guardini, *The Lord*. Chicago: Regnery Gateway, 1954, p. 302.

91 "*Thielicke*": Helmut Thielicke, *Waiting*, op. cit., p. 62.

92 "*Wilson*": Mark Noll, "Belfast: Tense with Peace" in *Books & Culture*, November/December 1995, p. 12.

93 "*O'Connor*": Elizabeth O'Connor, *Cry Pain*, op. cit., p. 50.

94 "*Time*": Lance Morrow, "I Spoke … As a Brother," in *Time*, January 9, 1984, pp. 27–33.

95 "*for they do not know*": Luke 23:34.

CHAPTER 8

97 "*Wink*": Walter Wink, *Engaging the Powers*. Minneapolis: Fortress, 1992, p. 275.

98 "*The Wages of Guilt*": Ian Buruma, *The Wages of Guilt: Memories of War in Germany and Japan*. New York: Farrar, Straus and Giroux, 1994.

99 "*We, the first*": Quoted in *Response*, a publication of the Simon Wiesenthal Center in Los Angeles.

114 "*Trueblood*": Elton Trueblood, *The Yoke of Christ*. Waco, Tex.: Word, 1958, p. 37.

117 "*Wink*": Walter Wink, *Engaging*, op. cit., p. 191.

118 "*Tutu*": Michael Henderson, *The Forgiveness Factor*. Salem, Ore.: Grosvenor Books USA, 1996, p. xix.

119 *"King"*: David Garrow, *Bearing the Cross*. New York: William Morrow, 1986, pp. 81, 500, 532.

120 *"van der Post"*: Laurens van der Post, *The Prisoner and the Bomb*. New York: William Morrow and Company, 1971, p. 133.

CHAPTER 9

121 *"Weil"*: Simone Weil, *Gravity*, op. cit., pp. 1, 16.

122 *"Barth"*: Karl Barth, *The Word of God and the Word of Man*. New York: Harper & Row, 1957, p. 92.

123 *"Merton"*: Thomas Merton, *No Man Is an Island*. New York: Harcourt, Brace and Company, 1955, p. 235.

124 *"Lewis"*: C. S. Lewis, *The Four Loves*. London: Geoffrey Bles, 1960, p. 149.

125 *"God in heaven"*: Quoted in Ernest Kurtz, *Spirituality*, op. cit., p. 29.

126 *"Then he turned"*: Luke 7:44 – 47.

127 *"Damnation"*: Harold Frederic, *The Damnation of Theron Ware*. New York: Penguin, 1956, pp. 75 –76.

128 *"Meyer"*: Quoted in Brennan Manning, *The Gentle Revolutionaries*. Denville, N.J.: Dimension, 1976, p. 66.

130 *"Mairs"*: Nancy Mairs, *Ordinary Time*, op. cit., p. 89.

135 *"Nietzsche"*: Quoted in Williams, *Singleness*, op. cit., p. 126.

136 *"Lewis"*: C. S. Lewis, *Mere*, op. cit., pp. 99 –100.

ABOUT THE
AUTHOR

Philip Yancey explores the most basic questions and deepest mysteries of the Christian faith, taking millions of readers with him. Early on he crafted bestselling books such as *Disappointment with God* and *Where Is God When It Hurts?* while also editing *The Student Bible*. More recently, he has felt the freedom to explore central issues of the Christian faith, penning award-winning titles such as *The Jesus I Never Knew, What's So Amazing About Grace?* (from which this material was taken), and *Prayer: Does It Make Any Difference?* His books have garnered thirteen Gold Medallion Awards from Christian publishers and booksellers. He currently has more than fifteen million books in print, published in more than fifty languages worldwide.

Yancey worked as a journalist in Chicago for some twenty years, editing the youth magazine *Campus Life* while also writing for a wide variety of magazines including *Reader's Digest*, *Saturday Evening Post*, *National Wildlife*, and *Christianity Today*. In the process he interviewed diverse people enriched by their personal faith, such as President Jimmy Carter, Habitat for Humanity founder Millard Fuller, and Dame Cicely Saunders, founder of the modern hospice movement.

In 1992 he and his wife Janet, a social worker and hospice chaplain, moved to the foothills of Colorado. His writing took a more personal, introspective turn even as his activities turned outward. "Writing is such an introspective act that I found myself looking for ways to connect with the planet bodily. My interests include skiing, climbing mountains, mountain-biking, golf, international travel, jogging, nature, theology (in small doses), politics, literature, and classical music."